Greek Prose Usage
A Companion to
Greek Prose Composition

Greek Prose Usage

A Companion to Greek Prose Composition

G.S. Thompson

Bristol Classical Press

First published in 1955 by Macmillan & Co. Ltd.

This edition published in 1998 by
Bristol Classical Press
an imprint of
Gerald Duckworth & Co. Ltd
The Old Piano Factory
48 Hoxton Square, London N1 6PB

© 1955 by G.S. Thompson

All rights reserved. No part of this publication
may be reproduced, stored in a retrieval system, or
transmitted, in any form or by any means, electronic,
mechanical, photocopying, recording or otherwise,
without the prior permission of the publisher.

A catalogue record for this book is available
from the British Library

ISBN 1-85399-554-1

Available in USA and Canada from:
Focus Information Group
PO Box 369
Newburyport
MA 01950

Printed in Great Britain by
Booksprint, Bristol

PREFACE

IT will be obvious that this is no more than a collection of notes on Greek prose usage, taken mainly from the works of Thucydides, Xenophon, Plato and Demosthenes. I began to make it some years ago when I could not find a handy reference book for my Sixth Form pupils; I hope it may be of use to others who feel the same need.

For all errors of fact or form I am alone to blame.

G. S. T.

CONTENTS

	PAGE
ORATIO RECTA	
Statements (including *Potential*)	1
Commands	2
Questions	3
ORATIO OBLIQUA	
Indirect Statements	7
Indirect Commands	13
Indirect Questions	13
Subordinate Clauses	15
VERBS OF HINDERING, DOUBTING, ETC.	17
VERBS OF PRECAUTION	18
VERBS OF FEARING	19
FINAL CLAUSES	21
CONSECUTIVE CLAUSES	23
CONDITIONAL SENTENCES	26
CONDITIONS IN ORATIO OBLIQUA	32
WISHES	36
TEMPORAL CLAUSES	37
CAUSAL CLAUSES	41
CONCESSIVE CLAUSES	43
COMPARATIVE CLAUSES	44
CORRELATIVES	49
RELATIVE CLAUSES	51
IMPERSONAL VERBS	57
THE USES OF THE PARTICIPLES	59

	PAGE
THE USES OF THE INFINITIVE	66
THE ADJECTIVE	71
THE ADVERB	76
THE ARTICLE	77
PRONOUNS	80
SUBJECT AND PREDICATE	87
APPOSITION	91
THE USES OF THE CASES	93
THE USES OF THE PREPOSITIONS	107
THE VERB	116
THE VERBAL ADJECTIVE	127
THE NEGATIVE	129
CONJUNCTIONS AND PARTICLES	132
ENGLISH INDEX	143
GREEK INDEX	147

ORATIO RECTA OR DIRECT SPEECH

A. STATEMENTS

The Indicative Mood is used to express a statement; the negative is οὐ.

But the statement may be modified with 'may', 'might', 'could', 'would' and the like in English, a use often called *potential*.

In Greek the optative with ἄν is used:

> ἔλθοι ἄν.
> He may (etc.) go.
>
> βουλοίμην ἄν + infinitive or accusative and infinitive.
> I should like, please.

This use is often much the same as a polite request or even an open future ('I shall'). The imperfect and aorist indicatives with ἄν mean 'would have', 'could have', 'might have' and the like:

> ἐβουλόμην ἄν, I should have liked.
> ἐπιστεύσατε ἄν, you might have believed.

These uses are similar to conditional apodoses, but the imperfect with ἄν referring to present time is uncommon in the potential sense.
But:

> ἐμοὶ ἂν ἐδόκει, I am inclined to think.

NOTES.—(i) This use must be distinguished from the iterative use of the imperfect with ἄν:

> διηρώτων ἄν, I used to ask.

(ii)
> ἆρ' ἐθελήσαις ἄν + infinitive, would you mind?
> ἡδέως ἄν + optative, I should like to.
> τάχα (τάχ') ἂν ἔλθοι, perhaps he will (may, would) come.
> τάχ' ἂν ἦλθεν, perhaps he would have (might have) come.

(iii) The imperfects ἔδει, (ἐ)χρῆν, ἐξῆν, without ἄν, are used with the infinitive to form a kind of potential expression :

> ἔδει σε τοῦτο ποιῆσαι, you should have done this.
> ἐξῆν σοι τοῦτο ποιῆσαι, you might have done this.

In these cases the non-fulfilment of the condition is definitely implied ('but you did not').

For the Participle of the Potential see Further Notes on Conditional Sentences and Notes on Participles.

A cautious assertion is expressed by μή with subjunctive :

> μὴ τοῦτο ἀληθὲς ᾖ, I rather think this is true.

A cautious negation is expressed by μή οὐ with subjunctive :

> μὴ οὐ τοῦτο χαλεπὸν ᾖ, perhaps it may not be difficult.
> μὴ οὐκ ᾖ διδακτόν, perhaps it is not teachable.

B. COMMANDS (in the 2nd and 3rd persons)

(i) *Affirmative.*—The imperative is used, present for general, aorist for particular commands :

> λέγε, speak.
> εἰπέ μοι, tell me.
> πείθου τοῖς νόμοις, obey the laws.
> ἀπελθέτω, let him go away.

The infinitive is sometimes found for imperative in Plato and Thucydides, more often in the poets.

(ii) *Negative.*—Use μή with the present imperative for a general prohibition, μή with the aorist subjunctive for a particular prohibition :

> μὴ κλέπτε, do not steal.
> μὴ ἀπέλθῃ, let him not go away.

Occasionally the aorist imperative is used in the 3rd person :

> μηδεὶς προσδοκησάτω, let no one expect.

GREEK PROSE USAGE

Commands (or exhortations) in the 1st person are expressed by the present or aorist subjunctive, with μή if negative ; they are often (almost always in 1st person singular) introduced by ἄγε or φέρε ('come !') :

(μή) ἀπέλθωμεν, let us (not) depart.

NOTES.—(i) Sometimes the future indicative (2nd person) is used for a command, with negative οὐ or μή :

ταύτην τὴν πίστιν φυλάξετε, hold on to this security.

This is especially common with ὅπως (negative μή). See Verbs of Precaution.

ὅπως μοι μὴ ἐρεῖς, don't tell me.

(ii) οὐ μή with future indicative (2nd person) expresses a strong prohibition, with the aorist subjunctive (usually 1st or 3rd person) an emphatic negation (the distinction is not always kept) :

οὐ μὴ ληρήσεις.
Don't talk nonsense.

οὐ μὴ παύσωμαι.
I will never cease.

οὐδέποτ' οὐδὲν μὴ γένηται.
Nothing will ever happen.

οὐδεὶς μηκέτι μείνῃ τῶν πολεμίων.
None of the enemy will remain any longer.

With δύναμαι and εἰμί the present subjunctive is found :

οὐ μή σοι δύνωνται ἀντέχειν οἱ πολέμιοι.
The enemy will not be able to resist you.

(iii) τί οὐ; is used for an exhortation :

τί οὐ σκοποῦμεν; let us consider.

C. QUESTIONS

The indicative is usually the mood (negative οὐ), introduced by an interrogative pronoun or adverb :

τίς εἶ; who are you ?

GREEK PROSE USAGE

If there is no interrogative word, the question may be indicated only by the sense (or the speaker's tone), but often particles are used as follows:

ἆρα or ἦ (chiefly poetical) for an open question.

ἆρ' οὐ
οὔκουν (*nōnne ergo?*) } for a question expecting the answer 'Yes'.

ἆρα μή or μή
μῶν or μῶν μή } for a question expecting the answer 'No'.
ἆρ' οὖν (*num igitur?*)

Alternative (or *Double*) *Questions* have ἤ for 'or' and have either no introductory particle or πότερον or πότερα.

'Or not' is ἢ οὔ; or ἢ μή;

A single question with ἤ is used following a more general question and suggesting the answer to it:

τίνα ταύτην; ἦ τὸ πλοῖον ἀφῖκται;
What message is this you bring? Is it that the ship has come?

NOTES.—(i) ἄλλο τι ἤ; or ἄλλο τι used for 'is it not?':

ἄλλο τι ἢ οὐδὲν κωλύει παριέναι;
Surely nothing prevents him from coming forward?
ἄλλο τι γεωργὸς μὲν εἷς;
Is it not (true) that one will be a farmer?

(ii) πῶς οὐ; in indignant or impatient questions:

πῶς οὐ δεινόν ἐστι; is it not disgraceful?

(iii) πῶς ἄν; + optative expresses a wish:

πῶς ἂν ἔλθοι; I wish he would come.

(iv)
τίς πόθεν εἶ; who are you and whence?

(v)
ἵνα τί ταῦτα λέγεις; for what purpose do you say this?
ἐπειδὰν τί γένηται; when what happens?

(vi)
τί τοῦτο ἔλεξας; what is this that you said?

GREEK PROSE USAGE

(vii) οὐκοῦν = 'therefore', with no negative significance. οὔκουν = 'not therefore'. Both may introduce questions.

(viii) καὶ πῶς expresses doubt or disbelief of what has just been stated. πῶς καί asks for additional information.

Deliberative Questions, mainly in the 1st person, are put in the subjunctive, present or aorist, and may be introduced by an interrogative pronoun or adverb or by βούλει, βούλεσθε, θέλεις (in poetry):

> τί εἴπω; what am I to say?
> βούλει εἴπω ταῦτα; am I to say this?

The negative is μή.

Deliberative questions in the 3rd person are found with the indefinite τις, meaning 'we' in general, but the construction with δεῖ is more usual. To translate 'what was I to do?' the imperfects ἔδει and (ἐ)χρῆν are used with the accusative and infinitive:

> τί ἔδει ἡμᾶς ποιεῖν; what were we to do?

Answers to questions can be expressed in many ways, *e.g.*:

YES	NO
μάλιστα	ἥκιστά γε
πῶς γὰρ οὔ;	οὐδαμῶς
πάνυ μὲν οὖν	οὐδείς, οὐδέποτε (giving a more
ναί	precise answer)
ἔγωγε (I do)	

NOTES.—(i) γάρ is used to mean 'Yes, no, for'.

> ἔστι γὰρ οὕτω, yes, for so it is.

(ii) The answer to ἄλλο τι ἤ; (= ἆρ' οὔ;) is:

> οὐδὲν ἄλλο, that is the case.

Exclamations. 'How' is ὡς, with adjectives and adverbs and verbs :

> ὡς ἀστεῖος ὁ ἀνήρ, how polite the man is!
> ὡς ὤνησας, how you helped me! how kind of you!

The pronouns are the same as the relatives : ὅσος, 'how great!', etc. There is no exclamation mark in Greek.

ORATIO OBLIQUA (INDIRECT OR REPORTED SPEECH)

(*Note.*—Conditions in Oratio Obliqua are under Conditional Sentences.)

A. STATEMENTS

(1) The accusative and infinitive construction (negative οὐ) is used after verbs of saying and thinking, particularly after φημί, οἴομαι (οἶμαι), ἡγέομαι, νομίζω, δοκέω. If the subject of the infinitive is the same as the subject of the verb of saying or thinking, it is in the nominative, though not expressed unless emphatic (αὐτός).

The tense of the infinitive is the same as that of the corresponding verb in the oratio recta.

Examples :

ἔφη τὸν ἀδελφὸν παρεῖναι.
He said his brother was present (my brother is present).

ἔφη (αὐτὸς) ποιῆσαι.
He said he (himself) had done it (I did it).

οὐκ ἔφη ποιήσειν.
He said he would not do it (I shall not do it).

NOTES.—(i)
    I say that . . . not, οὔ φημι.
    I think that . . . not, οὐκ οἴομαι, οὐ νομίζω.
    I hope not to, οὐκ ἐλπίζω.
    I wish not to, οὐ βούλομαι.

(ii) οἴομαι δεῖν (I think I must) is used as one verb with nominative and infinitive.

(iii) δοκέω ('I seem') is usually personal :

εὖ λέγειν μοι δοκεῖτε.
You seem to me to (it seems to me that you, I think that you) speak well.

δοκῶ μοι (or simply δοκῶ).
I think that I . . .

Used impersonally, δοκεῖ means 'it seems good':

δοκεῖ μοι, it seems good to me, I decide (with the infinitive).

(iv) Verbs of saying and thinking are often personal in the passive:

λέγεται ὁ Κῦρος, it is said that Cyrus . . .

but also λέγεται τὸν Κῦρον with the infinitive.

(v) The accusative of the reflexive pronoun, when used for the more usual nominative, is more emphatic:

ἡγησάμενος ἐμαυτὸν ἐπιεικέστερον εἶναι.
Thinking myself to be more reasonable.

(vi) For the negative in this construction see also Notes on the Negative.

(2) After λέγω (aorist εἶπον), the indirect statement is translated by ὅτι or ὡς with a finite verb (subject in the nominative); the same mood and tense are used as in the direct speech, negative οὐ.

NOTE.—ὅτι generally introduces a fact, ὡς the speaker's impression of it.

The ὅτι clause is continued with οὖν, ὥστε, γάρ, with the verb in the indicative or optative; but the nominative / accusative } and infinitive often takes its place:

ἀπεκρίναντο ὅτι ἀδύνατα σφίσιν εἴη . . . παῖδες γὰρ σφῶν εἶεν . . . δεδιέναι δέ . . .
They answered that it was impossible for them . . . for their children were . . ., and they feared . . .

This construction is common with other verbs of saying, like ἀποκρίνομαι, 'answer', ἀγγέλλω, 'announce' (also used with participle), but not with φημί:

εἶπεν
ἀπεκρίνατο } ὅτι οὐ ποιήσει (ποιήσοι).

He said (replied) that he would not do it (I shall not do it).

After a historic main verb the optative may be used in the ὅτι clause, both for indicative and subjunctive of oratio recta, but this change is not made with past indicatives in unreal conditions (see Conditions in Oratio Obliqua).

NOTE.—ὅτι may introduce the actual words of the speaker:

ἀπήγγειλεν ὅτι οἱ Λακεδαιμόνιοι κελεύουσιν ὑμᾶς.
He reported: 'The Lacedaemonians bid you'.

ἔφη ὅτι αὐτάρκης κόσμος μοί ἐστιν ἡ τοῦ ἀνδρὸς ἀρετή.
She said, 'My husband's valour is sufficient ornament for me'.

(3) With verbs of hoping, promising and swearing the future infinitive is used, with the subject, if expressed, in the nominative. Negative μή:

ὑπισχνοῦμαι μὴ αὐτὸς ἀπιέναι.
I promise not to go away myself.

NOTES.—(i) A 'that' clause after these verbs will take the accusative (or nominative) and infinitive, with the tense of direct speech; the negative is μή:

διομνύμενος μηδὲν εἶναι σοὶ καὶ Φιλίππῳ πρᾶγμα.
Swearing that you and Philip had nothing to do with each other.

(ii) The negative οὐ is found where it negatives a single word, e.g. οὔ φημι = 'I deny'.

(iii) Verbs of admitting, attesting, being convinced and the like are often used with negative μή (a 'confident assertion'):

ἐπεπείσμην μήτε γράφοντ' ἂν ἐμοῦ γράψαι βέλτιον μηδένα.
I was convinced that no one would move better resolutions than myself.

(iv) With ἐλπίζω and other verbs of saying and thinking the potential aorist infinitive with ἄν often stands for the future, expressing contingency as opposed to certainty (negative οὐ):

ἤλπιζεν τοὺς Ἀθηναίους οὐκ ἂν περιιδεῖν.
He hoped that the Athenians would not allow . . .

ἐνόμιζεν αὐτοὺς πλεῖστ' ἂν βλάπτειν . . . καὶ βεβαίους φύλακας ἔσεσθαι.

He thought they would be likely to do most injury and would be sure to prove strong guards.

The aorist infinitive with ἐλπίζω refers to the result immediately looked for:

ἤλπιζον χειρώσασθαι τὸ 'Ρήγιον.
They hoped to subdue Rhegium.

The phrases ἐλπίς ἐστι, 'there is hope', ἐν ἐλπίδι εἶναι, 'to be hopeful', ἐλπίδα ἔχειν, 'to have hope', have the future infinitive or potential aorist infinitive with ἄν or most often the aorist infinitive:

ἐν ἐλπίδι ἦν ἀναλαβεῖν τὴν πόλιν.
He was hopeful of capturing the city.

(v) ἦ μήν ('verily') is used with future infinitive after verbs of swearing:

ὤμοσαν ἦ μὴν βοηθήσειν.
They swore to bring help.

(4) With verbs of *knowing* and *perceiving* the accusative (or nominative) and participle construction is used:

οἶδα ἁμαρτών.
I know that I did wrong.

σύνοιδα ἐμαυτῷ ἁμαρτόντι (or ἁμαρτών).
I am conscious of having done wrong.

ᾔσθοντο τοὺς πολεμίους προσβαλοῦντας.
They perceived that the enemy would attack.

Such verbs are: οἶδα, γιγνώσκω, ἐπίσταμαι, 'know', ὁράω, 'see', αἰσθάνομαι, 'perceive', πυνθάνομαι, 'ascertain', εὑρίσκω, 'find out', ἀκούω, 'hear', δείκνυμι, φαίνω, δηλόω, ἀποφαίνω, 'show, point out', μέμνημαι, 'remember', ἐπιλανθάνομαι, 'forget', ἀγγέλλω, 'announce', σύνοιδα ἐμαυτῷ, 'I am conscious'.

NOTES.—(i) The construction with ὅτι or ὡς is used with many of these verbs, frequently with οἶδα and ἐπίσταμαι, and usually when the verb of knowing or perceiving is itself in the participle :

αἰσθόμενος ὅτι ἀπηχθόμην.
Perceiving that I had become hateful . . .

οἶδ' ὅτι (like δῆλον ὅτι), used in parenthesis, has the value of an adverb : 'surely', 'obviously', 'certainly' :

οὔτ' ἂν ὑμεῖς οἶδ' ὅτι ἐπαύσασθε πολεμοῦντες.
Nor would you certainly have stopped making war.

(ii) ἀγγέλλω and verbs meaning to learn and hear often have the accusative and infinitive (rarely verbs meaning to know) :

ἀκούω δ' εἶναι ἐν τῷ στρατεύματι Ῥοδίους.
I hear
I am told } that there are Rhodians in the army.

(iii) The genitive and participle is found with αἰσθάνομαι, 'perceive', ἀκούω, 'hear', μέμνημαι, 'remember', ἐπιλανθάνομαι, 'forget'. The genitive is used for something perceived by oneself, the accusative for something learnt by hearsay (the genitive of the object, the accusative of the object-clause) :

ἤκουσα αὐτοῦ διαλεγομένου.
I heard him conversing.
ἤκουσα αὐτὸν διαλεγόμενον.
I heard (they told me) that he was conversing.
ᾐσθόμην αὐτὸν ἐπιδημοῦντα.
I heard that he was in town.

(iv) οἶδα, ἐπίσταμαι with infinitive mean 'I know how to . . .'; ἐπιλανθάνομαι with infinitive means 'I forget to . . .'; μέμνημαι with infinitive means 'I remember to . . .':

μεμνήσθω ἀνὴρ ἀγαθὸς εἶναι, remember to be a good man.

(v) εὖ οἶδ' ὅτι, 'certainly', δῆλον ὅτι, 'obviously'.

(5) Verbs of emotion are followed by εἰ for 'that' with the indicative, negative μή. Such verbs are θαυμάζω,

'wonder', ἀγαπάω, 'rejoice'; αἰσχύνομαι, 'am ashamed', ἀγανακτέω, 'am indignant':

> θαυμάζω εἰ μηδεὶς ὀργίζεται.
> I am surprised that no one is angry.
>
> κατάπληξις οὐκ ὀλίγη εἰ πέρας μηδὲν ἔσται.
> No small perplexity that there is to be no end.

NOTES.—(i) The negative may be οὐ (cf. 3, note ii):

> ἀγανακτῶ εἰ Φίλιππος οὐ λυπεῖ.
> I am indignant that Philip fails to annoy.

(ii) ὅτι is used with these verbs in a causal sense ('because'). The negative is οὐ.

(iii) Do not confuse this use with that of the participle with these verbs, *e.g.*:

> θαυμάζω ἰδών σε, I am surprised { at seeing / to see } you.

(iv)
> θαυμάζω ὅπως ἠθέλησε.
> I wonder how it was that he was willing.

(6) No rules are laid down for the use of ὅτι, ὡς or the accusative and infinitive, *except that*:

- (1) φημί takes the accusative (or nominative) and infinitive.
- (2) λέγω, εἶπον, ἀποκρίνομαι usually have ὅτι (except λέγω in the passive). But

    > λέγω τὴν πόλιν παίδευσιν εἶναι.
    > I say that the city is an education . . .

- (3) Verbs meaning 'to think', *e.g.* οἴομαι, ἡγέομαι, νομίζω, δοκέω, usually take the accusative (or nominative) and infinitive.
- (4) Other affirmative *verba declarandi* take either ὅτι or the accusative (or nominative) and infinitive.
- (5) λέγω (chiefly in the passive) is used with the accusative and infinitive regularly when it

means 'they say', 'it is said'; when it means 'command' it takes the dative and infinitive.

B. Indirect Command

The infinitive (negative μή) is used to translate the English infinitive with verbs of asking, advising, commanding and the like. Such verbs are:

Tell, command, order	λέγω + dative, κελεύω + accusative
advise	παραινέω + dative
warn	νουθετέω + accusative
ask, beg	αἰτέω + accusative, ἀξιόω + accusative
claim	ἀξιόω
dissuade, forbid	οὐκ ἐάω + accusative

οὐκ εἴων ὑμᾶς προέσθαι, I was bidding you not to sacrifice.

The tense of the infinitive is usually present for continuous action, aorist for single action, but the distinction is not always made. The infinitive is usually active, with the subject often understood:

ξυνέδρους ἑλέσθαι ἐκέλευον.
They bade (them) choose commissioners.

Notes.—(i) οὐκ ἀξιόω may be used for ἀξιόω μή:

οὐκ ἀξιοῖ τιμωρεῖσθαι, he asks him not to punish.

(ii) The 3rd person singular imperative of oratio recta becomes infinitive when reported (*e.g.* in the terms of treaties):

ἢν δέ τις ἁλίσκηται, τοῦ λαβόντος εἶναι δοῦλον.
And that, if anyone is captured, he should be the slave of his captor. (Oratio recta: ἔστω δοῦλος.)

C. Indirect Question

The indirect interrogative pronoun or adverb introduces the indirect question; the verb is put in the same tense and mood as in oratio recta, but after a historic main verb the mood may be changed to optative.

[See note (iv).] The negative is the same as in oratio recta :

> ἠρόμην αὐτοὺς ὁπόθεν ἀφίκοιντο.
> I asked them where they had come from.

A single indirect question introduced by 'if' or 'whether' is translated by εἰ, the verb being in the same tense and mood as the oratio recta, or changed to optative after a historic main verb. The negative is either οὐ or μή.

A double indirect question takes ὁπότερον, πότερον (πότερα) followed by ἤ for 'or'. 'Or not' is ἤ οὐ or ἤ μή.

Examples of indirect questions :

> ἠρόμην αὐτὸν εἰ {βούλεται / βούλοιτο} ἐλθεῖν.
> I asked him if he wished to come.

> ἠρόμην αὐτὸν {πότερον βούλεται / ὁπότερον βούλοιτο} ἐλθεῖν {ἢ οὔ. / ἢ μή.}
> I asked him whether he wished to come or not.

> οὐκ οἶδα εἰ ἀπέλθω.
> I do not know if I am to go away.

NOTES.—(i) The direct interrogative word may be used and the mood not changed in historic sequence :

> ἠρόμην αὐτὸν τίς ἐστι, I asked him who he was.

(ii) The relatives ὅσος, οἷος, ὅς may introduce an indirect question :

> ὁρᾷς ἡμᾶς ὅσοι ἐσμέν; Do you see how many we are ?

(iii) εἰ is used for 'if' or 'whether', even with the subjunctive of deliberative question.

(iv) Past tenses of the indicative are usually not changed to optative in historic sequence. Conditional indicatives with ἄν are not changed.

(v) The subject of an indirect question is often put as

GREEK PROSE USAGE

the object of the main verb (accusativus *de quo* or anticipatory accusative) :

τοὺς Λακεδαιμονίους οὐ γιγνώσκω ὅ, τι βούλονται.
As for the Lacedaemonians, I do not know what they want.

So also with indirect statement :

ἐπιστάμενοι τὴν ἀπόβασιν ὅτι οὐκ ἂν βιάζοιτο.
Knowing about the landing that it could not be forced.

D. SUBORDINATE CLAUSES IN ORATIO OBLIQUA (see also Conditions in Oratio Obliqua)

(1) After a primary verb introducing oratio obliqua the verb in the subordinate clause is unchanged. After a historic verb the subordinate verb is commonly changed from indicative to optative or from ἄν with subjunctive to optative without ἄν, but not a verb in the aorist indicative :

ἀπεκρίνατο ὅτι βουλεύσοιτο ὅτι δύναιτο ἀγαθόν.
He replied that he would plan whatever good he could.

But

ἠρόμην εἴ τινες εἶεν μάρτυρες ὧν ἐναντίον ἀπέδοσαν.
I asked if there were any witnesses in whose presence they had paid the money.

The vivid use of the form of oratio recta is, of course, possible :

ἀπεκρινάμην ὅτι μοι λυσιτελοῖ ὥσπερ ἔχω ἔχειν.
I replied that it was better for me to be as I was.

(2) This is true also of virtual oratio obliqua, especially with εἰ = 'to see if, in case', ὅτι = 'on the ground that', ἕως = 'until', where the use of the optative after a historic main verb shows the virtual oratio obliqua. See also Further Notes on Conditional Sentences (iii) :

ἀποστέλλει ἄνδρα ἐς τὰς Ἀθήνας εἴ τι ἄρα ἐνδοῖεν.
He despatched a man to Athens, to see if they would surrender.

ἔδοξεν αὐτοῖς πειρᾶσαι εἰ δύναιντο.
They decided to try, if haply they could.

NOTE.—A relative or adverb clause in oratio obliqua may be attracted to the accusative and infinitive :

> τοῦτον μυθολογοῦσι δακτύλιον φέρειν, ὃν περιελόμενον ἐκβῆναι.
>
> This man, they relate, was wearing a ring, which (the shepherd) took off and went away.
>
> ἐπειδὴ δ' οὖν πάσας τὰς ψυχὰς τοὺς βίους ᾑρῆσθαι, προσιέναι πρὸς τὴν Λάχεσιν.
>
> Then, he said, when all the souls had chosen their lives, they went to Lachesis.

VERBS OF HINDERING, PREVENTING, FORBIDDING, DOUBTING AND DENYING

THESE verbs take the infinitive with μή; if they are negative, they take the infinitive with μή οὐ:

> εἴργω σε μὴ τοῦτο ποιεῖν.
> I prevent you from doing this.
>
> οὐκ εἴργω σε μὴ οὐ τοῦτο ποιεῖν.
> I do not prevent you from doing this.

Such verbs are:

ἀρνοῦμαι, deny.
ἀπαγορεύω (aor. ἀπεῖπον), forbid.
ἀποψηφίζομαι, vote against.
κωλύω, prevent.

ἐμποδών εἰμι, hinder.
ἐναντιοῦμαι, oppose.
εἴργω, prevent.
ἀπέχω, hold off.

NOTES.—(i) κωλύω usually takes simple infinitive.

(ii) Present and aorist infinitives are used, but with verbs of denying the aorist has a past meaning:

> ἐξαρνεῖται μὴ λαβεῖν, he denies having received.

(iii) A genitive of the article and infinitive may be used with μή, but not with μὴ οὐ:

> (οὐκ) εἴργω σε τοῦ μὴ τοῦτο ποιεῖν.
> I (do not) prevent you from doing this.

(iv) The infinitive with τὸ μή (τὸ μὴ οὐ) is also used:

> οὐδὲν αὐτοὺς ἐπιλύεται ἡ ἡλικία τὸ μὴ οὐχὶ ἀγανακτεῖν.
> Their age does not save them from being distressed.

VERBS OF PRECAUTION AND STRIVING

THESE verbs take ὅπως (μή) with the subjunctive or, more frequently, the future indicative. The future indicative is usually unchanged in historic time, but the future optative is found.

Such verbs are:

ἐπιμελοῦμαι, take care.
εὐλαβοῦμαι, take care.
μέλει μοι, it is a care to me.
σπουδάζω, am eager.
μηχανῶμαι, contrive.
παρασκευάζομαι, prepare.

πράττω, arrange.
ὁράω, see to it.
σκοπέω, see to it.
φυλάττομαι, am on my guard.
φροντίζω, am anxious.

NOTES.—(i) φροντίζω, 'I am anxious', and ὅρα, 'beware', are followed also by μή (μὴ οὐ) with subjunctive or optative (see Verbs of Fearing).

(ii)
> ἐφυλάξαντο μὴ παθεῖν.
> They were on their guard against suffering.

So occasionally other verbs of precaution take the infinitive.

(iii) If the verb of precaution is in the imperative and its subject is also that of the subordinate verb, it is often omitted; the ὅπως clause is equivalent to a command or prohibition:

> ὅπως (μὴ) τοῦτο ποιήσεις, mind you do (don't do) this.

(iv) ὁρῶ, σκοπῶ can be followed by εἰ ('if, whether'). See Indirect Questions.

VERBS OF FEARING

THERE are three constructions:

(1) FEARS FOR THE FUTURE.—μή, 'that, lest', μὴ οὐ, 'that not', with the subjunctive in primary time, the optative in historic time:

φοβοῦμαι μὴ εὕρωμεν, I am afraid that we may find.

We also find μή and ὅπως μή with the future indicative. This emphasizes the realization of the fear:

φοβοῦμαι μὴ εὑρήσομεν, I suspect we shall find.

(2) FEARS FOR THE PRESENT AND PAST.—μή, μὴ οὐ with the indicative:

φοβοῦμαι μὴ τέθνηκεν, I am afraid that he is dead.

(3) With the infinitive, as in English, sometimes with the article:

φοβοῦμαι (τὸ) ἀποθανεῖν, I am afraid to die, I fear death.

NOTES.—(i) When 'I am afraid of' means 'I have not the courage to' (*prae timōre nōlō*), use the infinitive: otherwise use μή.

(ii) The future optative is *not* used for a future fear in historic time.

(iii) Words implying danger and the like take this construction, as also ὑποπτεύω, 'I suspect', ὀκνῶ, 'I hesitate'.

But κινδυνεύω takes the infinitive:

ἐκινδύνευσεν ἂν διαφθαρῆναι.
It would have been in danger of being destroyed.

Note also κινδυνεύω εἶναι, 'I probably am'.

(iv) For the elliptic use of μή and μὴ οὐ see Direct Statements.

(v) An indirect question occasionally follows a verb of fearing:

> οὐ δέδοικα εἰ Φίλιππος ζῇ (*pres. indic.*).
> I am not afraid if Philip is alive.

(vi) A causal clause with ὅτι, 'because', may follow a verb of fearing.

(vii) μὴ πολλάκις = 'lest perchance':

ὑποτοπήσας μὴ πολλάκις τοὺς ἀγροὺς παραλίπῃ.
Suspecting that he might perchance pass by his estate . . .

FINAL CLAUSES

PURPOSE is expressed by ἵνα, ὡς, ὅπως with the subjunctive in primary sequence, the optative in historic sequence. Negative μή:

διανοεῖται τὴν γέφυραν λῦσαι, ἵνα μὴ διαβῆτε.
He intends to destroy the bridge, that you may not cross.

NOTES.—(i) μή (= 'for fear lest') is used with subjunctive or optative for a negative purpose. Negative οὐ.

(ii) ὅπως (μή) with the future indicative, as with verbs of precaution, sometimes expresses a final clause:

οἱ σύμμαχοι οὐδὲ δι' ἓν ἄλλο τρέφονται ἢ ὅπως μαχοῦνται.
The allies are being maintained for one purpose only, that they may fight.

(iii) ἄν is sometimes used with ὡς, ὅπως and the subjunctive, e.g.:

ὡς ἂν μάθῃς, that you may learn.

But where ἵνα ἄν occurs, it means 'wherever'.

(iv) ἵνα is the usual conjunction (except ὅπως in Thucydides).

(v) ἵνα with the past tenses of the indicative expresses an unfulfilled purpose:

καὶ μὴν ἄξιόν γ' ἦν ἀκοῦσαι, ἵνα ἤκουσας ἀνδρῶν διαλεγομένων.
Yet it would have been worth while listening, that you might have heard men conversing.

(vi) The present subjunctive and optative is used for continuous or repeated action.

The aorist subjunctive and optative is used for momentary or single action.

(vii) Other ways of expressing a purpose are :
- (a) The future participle.
- (b) The infinitive.
- (c) The relative pronoun.
- (d) The genitive of the article with infinitive.

CONSECUTIVE CLAUSES

(1) ὥστε, preceded by οὕτως, 'so', τοσοῦτον, 'so much' and the like is used with the infinitive or accusative and infinitive to translate a consecutive 'that' or 'as to'. The negative is μή.

NOTE.—Where the negative οὐ is found, it is usually due to the fact that the infinitive after ὥστε is an oblique infinitive representing a direct indicative :

ἀκούω τοὺς Λακεδαιμονίους . . . ἂν ἀναχωρεῖν, ὥστ' οὐδὲ χρημάτων ὠνεῖσθαι παρ' οὐδενὸς οὐδέν.
I hear that the Lacedaemonians used to retreat . . . and so used to buy nothing from anyone.

(2) It is used with the indicative (or potential optative) when the consequence is an actual fact, particularly with narrative statements in the aorist.
The negative is οὐ :

(1) οὕτως ἐστὶ δεινὸς ὥστε δίκην μὴ διδόναι.
He is so clever as not to be punished.
(2) οὕτως ἐστὶ δεινὸς ὥστε δίκην οὐ δίδωσι.
He is so clever that he is not punished.

(3) When ὥστε as a connecting relative means 'so that', 'consequently', 'and so', without οὕτως or the like preceding, the indicative is used :

ὥστε κάκωσις ἐγένετο, therefore distress was caused.

(4) ἐφ' ᾧ and ἐφ' ᾧτε are used to mean 'on condition that', with the (accusative and) infinitive or the future indicative. The negative is μή in both uses :

ξυνέβησαν ἐφ' ᾧ μὴ ἀδικεῖν τοὺς Ἕλληνας.
They came to terms on condition that they did not harm the Greeks.

Notice that the *future* infinitive is not used except where the infinitive after ὥστε is due to the oblique form of the whole sentence:

μωρία τὰ τοιαῦτ' ἐλπίζειν ... ὥστε μηδὲν δεινὸν πείσεσθαι.
It is folly to hope for such things and so to escape any danger.

Here οὐδέν would be more usual.
We also find:

ξυνέβησαν ὥστε παραδοῦναι, they agreed to hand over ...

NOTES.—(i) ὥστε with the (accusative and) infinitive can mean 'that so' and with the negative 'to avoid'. It is indistinguishable in this use from ἵνα μή:

πᾶν ποιοῦσιν ὥστε μὴ δίκην διδόναι.
They do anything so as not to pay (to avoid paying) the penalty.

(ii) ὥστε with the participle is found after verbs of perception:

ὁρῶ τὸν ἐν ἡλικίᾳ οὕτω διακείμενον ὥστε οὐ φάσκοντα.
I see the young so disposed as to deny ...

(οὔ φημι is treated as one word; hence negative οὐ.)

(iii) οἷος = ὥστε:

ἐγὼ τοιοῦτος οἷος μηδενὶ πείθεσθαι.
I am such a man as to obey no one.

(iv) So the relative after τοιοῦτος, equal to ὥστε with the demonstrative. Negative μή:

ἔπραξε γὰρ οὗτος τοιαῦτα δι' ἃ νῦν μισεῖται.
For he did such things that he is now hated for them.

(v) The infinitive with ἄν after ὥστε represents a direct optative with ἄν:

ὥστε ἥδιστα ἂν σφᾶς αὐτοὺς ῥίπτειν ...
So that they would most gladly throw themselves ...

(vi) ὡς with infinitive is found for ὥστε:

ὡς πλεονεκτοῦντας δίκην μὴ διδόναι.
So as to avoid paying the penalty by fraud.

(vii) ὅσον = ὥστε:

ἐλείπετο τῆς νυκτὸς ὅσον σκοταίους διελθεῖν.
So much of the night was left as to enable them to pass through in the dark.

CONDITIONAL SENTENCES

They consist of an 'if' clause (protasis) and a main clause (apodosis).

A. Present Suppositions

(1) Particular : εἰ + present indicative ;
    present indicative :

εἰ ἡσυχίαν ἄγει, οὐκέτι δεῖ λέγειν.
If he is at peace, there is no longer need to speak.

(2) General : ἐάν (ἤν or ἄν) + subjunctive (present or aorist) ;
    present indicative :

ἐὰν ἔλθῃ θάνατος, οὐδεὶς βούλεται ἀποθανεῖν.
If (ever) death comes, no one is (ever) willing to die.

(3) Unfulfilled : εἰ + imperfect indicative ;
    ἄν + imperfect indicative :

εἰ ἐτιμῶντο, θαυμαστότερον ἂν ἦν.
If they were being honoured it would be more wonderful.

B. Past Suppositions

(1) Particular : εἰ + past indicative ;
    past indicative :

εἰ θεοῦ ἦν, οὐκ ἦν αἰσχροκερδής.
If he was the son of a god, he was not avaricious.

(2) General : εἰ + optative (present or aorist) ;
    imperfect indicative :

εἴ τινας θορυβουμένους αἴσθοιτο, κατασβεννύναι τὴν ταραχὴν ἐπειρᾶτο.
If (ever) he saw any falling into disorder, he tried (would try) to quiet the confusion.

(3) Unfulfilled : εἰ + aorist indicative ;
ἄν + aorist indicative :

καὶ ἴσως ἂν ἀπέθανον, εἰ μὴ ἡ ἀρχὴ κατελύθη.
Perhaps I should have perished, had not the government been put down.

C. Future Suppositions

(1) Open : ἐάν + subjunctive (present or aorist) ;
future indicative ;
or : εἰ + future indicative ;
future indicative :

ἐὰν ἴῃς νῦν, πότε ἔσει οἴκοι;
If you go now, when will you be at home?

μᾶλλον ἔτι μισοῦμαι, οὐ δικαίως, εἰ μὴ ἐμοὶ ἀναθήσετε.
I am the more hated, not rightly . . . unless you are going to attribute it to me.

(2) Vague : εἰ + optative (present or aorist) ;
ἄν + optative (present or aorist) :

εἰ ἴοις νῦν, πότ' ἂν εἴης οἴκοι;
If you were to go now, when would you be at home?

NOTES.—(i) The negative in the protasis is μή, in the apodosis οὐ.

(ii) εἰ + future indicative in an open future condition usually means 'if you are going to', 'if you intend to' (εἰ μέλλεις + future infinitive).

(iii) The protasis and apodosis in the same kind of condition (*i.e.* particular, general or unfulfilled) may refer to different times, each taking the appropriate tense :

εἰ ἔπραξε (πράσσει) τοῦτο, καλῶς εἶχεν (ἔχει, ἕξει).
If he did (does) this, it was (is, will be) well.

εἰ ἔπραξε τοῦτο, καλῶς ἂν εἶχεν.
If he had done this, it would now be well.

(iv) The apodosis may be an imperative, a subjunctive of exhortation or prohibition, or an optative of wish.

NOTES ON GENERAL CONDITIONS.—(i) These conditions are indefinite where 'if' = 'if ever', and they are used in the present or past.

(ii) 'Would' in the apodosis in past time means 'used to', and is to be distinguished from 'would' in the apodosis of unfulfilled and vague conditions.

(iii) The apodosis in past time (general) may be translated by ἄν with the imperfect indicative (iterative use):

> διηρώτων ἄν τοὺς ἀεὶ προσιόντας.
> They used to question everyone they met.

Also with imperfect infinitive in oratio obliqua:

> ἀκούω τοὺς Λακεδαιμονίους . . . ἄν ἀναχωρεῖν.
> I hear that the Lacedaemonians used to retreat.

(iv) The construction of general conditions is also used with relative pronouns and adverbs (q.v.).

FURTHER NOTES ON CONDITIONAL SENTENCES.—(i) In a protasis, instead of negative μή, we find οὔ φημι, 'I deny', οὐ πολλοί, 'a few', and the like, where οὐ is kept as connected with a particular word.

(ii) 'But if not (otherwise)' is εἰ δὲ μή, even if ἐάν precedes, or after a negative:

> μὴ ποιήσῃς ταῦτα· εἰ δὲ μή, αἰτίαν ἕξεις.
> Don't do this; otherwise, you will be blamed.
>
> ἐάν τι δέῃ· εἰ δὲ μή . . .
> If need be; otherwise . . .

'Unless, except' is εἰ μή, πλὴν εἰ, εἰ μὴ εἰ, ὅτι μή:

> οὐδὲν ἐπράχθη, εἰ μὴ εἴ τι πρὸς περιοίκους.
> Nothing was done, except against neighbours.
>
> οὐ παρεγένοντο ὅτι μὴ ὀλίγοι.
> Only a few appeared.

ἀλλ' ἤ means 'except' after a negative or virtual negative:

> τίνες ἄλλοι καταλείπονται ἀλλ' ἢ οἱ ἄδικοι;
> What others are left, except the unjust?

'Whether . . . or' is εἴτε (ἐάντε) . . . εἴτε (ἐάντε).

GREEK PROSE USAGE

See Concessive Clauses
- 'Even if' is καὶ εἰ (ἐάν), κἂν εἰ (καὶ ἂν εἰ).
- 'Not even if' is οὐδ' εἰ (ἐάν).
- 'Although' is εἰ καί.

'*Nisi forte*' (ironical) is εἰ μὴ ἄρα.

'If after all' is ἐάν (εἰ) ἄρα, implying an unlikely contingency :

ἢν ἄρα μὴ πρότερον ἕλωσιν, if they *should* fail to take it . . .

'If by chance' is ἐάν (εἰ) πολλάκις.

(iii) ἐάν πως with subjunctive, εἴ πως with optative are used as virtual conditions, where the apodosis has to be supplied from the context. The meaning is : 'if haply, to see if, in case, in the hope that', etc., and the clause is in virtual oratio obliqua :

βούλει δεώμεθα, ἐάν πως ἐνδειξώμεθα;
Are we to ask, to see if we can prove . . . ?

πρὸς τὴν πόλιν ἐχώρουν, εἴ πως ἐπιβοηθοῖεν.
They advanced to the city, in case (the citizens) should make a sally.

ὑποφειδόμενοι, εἴ πως ἐθελήσειαν διιέναι αὐτούς.
Acting with restraint, in the hope that they should let them pass through.

(iv) The imperfects ἔδει, χρῆν (ἐχρῆν), ἐξῆν, εἰκὸς ἦν and neuter adjectives with ἦν omit ἄν in unfulfilled conditions : ἔδει with present infinitive = 'ought to' ; ἔδει with aorist infinitive = 'ought to have' :

εἰ πάντες ὡμολογοῦμεν . . ., οὐδὲν ἄλλο ἔδει τὸν παριόντα λέγειν.
If we all agreed . . ., a speaker ought to say nothing else.

ἐπεὶ βραχὺς καὶ σαφὴς ἐξήρκει λόγος.
For a short and clear speech had been sufficient.

καλὸν δ' ἦν, εἰ καὶ ἡμαρτάνομεν, τοῖσδε εἶξαι.
It would have been honourable for these men to yield, although we were at fault.

Compare the use of ὤφελον in Wishes (*q.v.*).

ἂν ἔδει means 'it would be necessary, there would be need' :

οὐδὲν ἂν ὑμᾶς νῦν ἔδει βουλεύεσθαι.
There would be no need for you to be deliberating now.

(v) An unfulfilled purpose in past time is expressed by ἵνα, ὡς, ὅπως with imperfect or aorist indicative :

οὐκοῦν, εἴπερ ἀληθὲς ἦν, ἐχρῆν τὸ γραμματεῖον εἰς τὸν ἐχῖνον ἐμβαλεῖν, ἵνα οἱ δικασταὶ τὸ πρᾶγμα ἔγνωσαν;
Then, if this were true, ought he not to have put the ledger in the box, that so the jury might have understood the matter ?

(vi) ὥσπερ εἰ, ὥσπερ ἂν εἰ, mean 'like'. See Comparative Clauses.

(vii) The position of ἄν is before the verb, where emphasis is on words before the verb, *e.g.* an interrogative or negative : πῶς ἄν; or οὐκ ἄν. Otherwise it is put directly after the verb.

(viii) οὐκ οἶδα ἂν εἰ, οὐκ ἂν οἶδα εἰ with the optative mean 'perhaps' :

Perhaps I $\begin{Bmatrix} \text{can} \\ \text{could} \end{Bmatrix}$ οὐκ ἂν οἶδα εἰ δυναίμην = οὐκ οἶδα εἰ δυναίμην ἄν.

(ix) The optative with ἄν in apodosis may be potential, equal to less emphatic present or future and followed by εἰ with present indicative :

πολλὴ ἄν με φιλοψυχία ἔχοι, εἰ οὕτως ἀλόγιστός εἰμι.
I am very fond of life, if I am so unreasonable.

Similarly the potential optative with ἄν may occur in the protasis :

οὐδ' εἰ μὴ ποιήσαιτ' ἂν τοῦτο.
Not even if you would not do this.

(x) A relative clause in a condition has the tense or mood of its verb attracted to that of the condition :

θαυμαστὴ ἂν εἴη ἡ διατριβὴ ὁπότε ἐντύχοιμι.
Marvellous would be the sojourn there, when I should meet (= when I shall meet).

(Optative in vague future condition.)

οὐκ ἂν ἐπαυόμην ἕως ἀπεπειράθην.
I should not have stopped, until I had made trial.

GREEK PROSE USAGE

(xi) The perfect is sometimes used (for future) of something bound to happen if the condition is fulfilled:

τὰ πράγματα κεκώλυται εἰ μὴ αὐτὸς παρέσομαι.
Things are bound to be held up if I myself am not there.

(xii) The pluperfect with ἄν refers to something that would have been completed in the past and have remained so up to the present :

ὥστε τῆς εἰρήνης ἂν διημαρτήκει.
So that he would finally have missed the peace (and still have been without it).

(xiii) Omission of ἄν in apodosis, when it expresses a necessary or vivid consequence :

ὧν κατορθουμένων μεγίστοις ὑπῆρχεν ἡμῖν εἶναι.
If these measures had been successful, it was within our reach to be the greatest people.

(xiv) The optative in protasis is used idiomatically in proverbial expressions, to put the case in a more general way than the indicative :

ἀνδρῶν σωφρόνων ἐστίν, εἰ μὴ ἀδικοῖντο, ἡσυχάζειν.
Prudent men keep quiet, unless they be injured.

(xv) εἴπερ, ἐάνπερ, 'if really, if as is the fact' :

ταῦτα ἐπιψήφιζε, εἴπερ ἡγεῖ σοι προσήκειν . . .
Put this to the vote, if (since) you think it your duty . . .

(xvi) ἄν with the participle (the participle of the potential) :

περὶ μεγίστης καὶ ὀνομαστοτάτης πασῶν ἂν πράξεως οὔσης . . .
About a very great deed and one which would have been most famous of all.

καὶ αὐτοὶ ἥδιον ἂν ὁρῶντες (ἥδιον ἂν ὁρῷεν).
Because they themselves would be pleased to see . . .

πόλλ' ἂν ἔχων εἰπεῖν.
Though I could say much.

CONDITIONS IN ORATIO OBLIQUA

(1) AFTER ὅτι, ὡς, the direct form of the condition is kept in primary time, except for changes of person and the like. After a historic main verb, the indicative may be changed to optative and ἐάν with subjunctive to εἰ with optative.

But (i) do not change the *tense* of direct speech; (ii) do not change past indicatives in unfulfilled conditions to optative, either in protasis or apodosis.

The same rules apply to indirect questions. For examples see below.

(2) With the accusative (nominative) and infinitive construction, it is the apodosis which has the verb in the infinitive.

- (a) In open conditions, the tense of the infinitive is the same as the tense of the indicative in oratio recta.
- (b) In unfulfilled conditions, ἄν with present infinitive stands for ἄν with imperfect indicative and present optative; ἄν with aorist infinitive stands for ἄν with aorist indicative and aorist optative.

The protasis follows the rule of (1) above. For examples see below.

(3) With the participle construction, the rule is as in (2) above, using the participle for the infinitive. For examples see below.

NOTES.—(i) By the vivid construction, the tense and mood of oratio recta may be kept, even in historic time:

προηγόρευεν αὐτοῖς ὡς εἰ μὴ ἐκπέμψοιεν τοὺς Λακεδαιμονίους πόλεμον ἐξοίσει.

He announced to them that if they did not dismiss the Spartans he would make war.

GREEK PROSE USAGE

(ii) As already said, past indicatives in unfulfilled conditions are *not* changed to optative.

(iii) ἄν is often attached to the governing verb when followed by accusative and infinitive or participle :

οὐκ ἄν μοι δοκῶ, I don't think I should.

(iv) It is probable that only the *future* indicative in a protasis is changed to optative in oratio obliqua, so that the optative (except future) represents either ἐάν with subjunctive or εἰ with optative of oratio recta. In other words, εἰ with present or aorist indicative in oratio recta is not changed to optative in oratio obliqua.

(v) Virtual oratio obliqua :

διδόντος τοῦ Τιθραύστου πολλὰ δῶρα, εἰ ἀπέλθοι.
When Tithraustes offered him many gifts, if he would depart.
(Oratio recta : I will give you many gifts, ἐὰν ἀπέλθῃς.)

Very commonly in a final clause after ὅπως :

ἔταξαν εἴκοσι ναῦς, ὅπως, εἰ ἄρα ὁ Φορμίων παραπλέοι, οἱ Ἀθηναῖοι μὴ διαφύγοιεν.
They drew up twenty ships, in order that, if Phormio should sail past, the Athenians should not escape.
(Oratio recta: ἐὰν ὁ Φορμίων παραπλέῃ, οἱ Ἀθηναῖοι διαφυγεῖν οὐ δυνήσονται.)

EXAMPLES OF CONDITIONS IN ORATIO OBLIQUA

Present Particular :

εἰ τοῦτο ποιοῦσιν ἁμαρτάνουσιν.
If they are doing this, they are doing wrong.

εἶπεν ὅτι   εἰ τοῦτο { ποιοῖεν ἁμαρτάνοιεν.
                         ποιοῦσιν ἁμαρτάνουσιν.

ἔφη αὐτοὺς   εἰ τοῦτο { ποιοῖεν
                         ποιοῦσιν } ἁμαρτάνειν.

ᾔσθετο αὐτοὺς εἰ τοῦτο { ποιοῖεν
                          ποιοῦσιν } ἁμαρτάνοντας.

Present Unfulfilled:

εἰ τοῦτο ἐποίουν, ἡμάρτανον ἄν.
If they were doing this, they would be doing wrong.

εἶπεν ὅτι εἰ τοῦτο ἐποίουν ἡμάρτανον ἄν.
ἔφη αὐτοὺς εἰ τοῦτο ἐποίουν ἁμαρτάνειν ἄν.
ᾔσθετο αὐτοὺς εἰ τοῦτο ἐποίουν ἁμαρτάνοντας ἄν.

Past Particular:

εἰ τοῦτο ἐποίησαν ἥμαρτον.
If they did this, they did wrong.

εἶπεν ὅτι εἰ τοῦτο ἐποίησαν ἥμαρτον (ἁμάρτοιεν).
ἔφη αὐτοὺς εἰ τοῦτο ἐποίησαν ἁμαρτεῖν.
ᾔσθετο αὐτοὺς εἰ τοῦτο ἐποίησαν ἁμαρτόντας.

Past Unfulfilled:

εἰ τοῦτο ἐποίησαν ἥμαρτον ἄν.
If they had done this, they would have done wrong.

εἶπεν ὅτι εἰ τοῦτο ἐποίησαν ἥμαρτον ἄν.
ἔφη αὐτοὺς εἰ τοῦτο ἐποίησαν ἁμαρτεῖν ἄν.
ᾔσθετο αὐτοὺς εἰ τοῦτο ἐποίησαν ἁμαρτόντας ἄν.

Future Open:

$\begin{cases} ἐὰν\ τοῦτο\ ποιήσωσιν \\ εἰ\ τοῦτο\ ποιήσουσιν \end{cases}$ ἁμαρτήσονται.

If they do this, they will do wrong.

εἶπεν ὅτι ἐὰν τοῦτο ποιήσωσιν ἁμαρτήσονται.

εἶπεν ὅτι $\begin{cases} εἰ\ τοῦτο\ ποιήσειαν \\ εἰ\ τοῦτο\ ποιήσουσιν \\ εἰ\ τοῦτο\ ποιήσοιεν \end{cases}$ ἁμαρτήσοιντο.

ἔφη αὐτοὺς $\begin{cases} εἰ\ τοῦτο\ ποιήσειαν \\ εἰ\ τοῦτο\ ποιήσουσιν \\ εἰ\ τοῦτο\ ποιήσοιεν \end{cases}$ ἁμαρτήσεσθαι.

ᾔσθετο αὐτοὺς $\begin{cases} εἰ\ τοῦτο\ ποιήσειαν \\ εἰ\ τοῦτο\ ποιήσουσιν \\ εἰ\ τοῦτο\ ποιήσοιεν \end{cases}$ ἁμαρτησομένους.

Future Vague:

εἰ τοῦτο ποιοῖεν ἁμαρτάνοιεν ἄν.
If they were to be doing this, they would be doing wrong.

εἰ τοῦτο ποιήσειαν ἁμάρτοιεν ἄν.
If they were to do this, they would do wrong.

εἶπεν ὅτι { εἰ τοῦτο ποιοῖεν ἁμαρτάνοιεν ἄν.
{ εἰ τοῦτο ποιήσειαν ἁμάρτοιεν ἄν.
ἔφη αὐτοὺς εἰ τοῦτο ποιοῖεν ἁμαρτάνειν ἄν.
ᾔσθετο αὐτοὺς εἰ τοῦτο ποιοῖεν ἁμαρτάνοντας ἄν.
ἔφη αὐτοὺς εἰ τοῦτο ποιήσειαν ἁμαρτεῖν ἄν.
ᾔσθετο αὐτοὺς εἰ τοῦτο ποιήσειαν ἁμαρτόντας ἄν.

WISHES

(1) FOR THE FUTURE.—εἴθε (εἰ γάρ) + optative (present or more commonly aorist):

> εἴθε μὴ γένοιτο, may it not happen!

(2) FOR THE PRESENT.—εἴθε (εἰ γάρ) + imperfect indicative:

> εἰ γὰρ ὁ Κῦρος ἔζη, would that Cyrus were alive!

(3) FOR THE PAST.—εἴθε (εἰ γάρ) + aorist indicative:

> εἴθε τοῦτο ἔπραξεν, would that he had done this!

NOTES.—(i) The negative is μή.

(ii) εἴθε, εἰ γάρ may be omitted in (1), but not in (2) and (3).

(iii) ὤφελον, 'I ought', 2nd aorist of ὀφείλω, 'I owe', is used with present or aorist infinitive to express a wish that cannot be fulfilled. The negative (with the infinitive) is μή and εἴθε, εἰ γάρ often introduce the wish:

> εἴθ' ὤφελε (μὴ) τοῦτο ποιεῖν.
> Would that he were (not) doing this!
> εἴθ' ὤφελε (μὴ) τοῦτο ποιῆσαι.
> Would that he had (not) done this!

This construction is *personal*:

> εἴθ' ὤφελε Κῦρος ζῆν, would that Cyrus were alive!

TEMPORAL CLAUSES

(1) THESE clauses, if expressing a definite fact, have the verb in the indicative (usually a past tense):

ἐπειδὴ ἀφίκοντο, when they (had) arrived.

(Note aorist for English pluperfect.)

A participle often translates a temporal clause; the English present often needs the aorist in Greek: 'hearing this' is usually ταῦτα ἀκούσας. The present in Greek is to be used if the English means when or while doing something. See also The Uses of the Participles.

(2) If a temporal clause refers to the future, it takes the indefinite construction (the prospective use): ἄν + subjunctive (present or aorist) in primary sequence; optative (present or aorist) without ἄν in historic sequence:

ὅταν ἀπιέναι καιρὸς δοκῇ, σὺν σοὶ ἡμᾶς ἄγε.
When it seems time to depart, take us with you.

μενῶ ἕως ἂν ἔλθῃ.
I shall wait until he comes (for him to come).

ἔμενον ἕως ἔλθοι.
I waited until he should come (for him to come).

(Do *not* use the *future* optative here.)

(3) A temporal clause may be general or indefinite, expressing customary action ('when' = 'whenever'). ἄν + subjunctive (present or aorist) in primary sequence; optative (present or aorist) without ἄν in historic sequence. (Compare 'if ever' in a general condition and 'whoever' in a general relative clause):

ὅταν } ἔλθῃ θάνατος, οὐδεὶς βούλεται θνῄσκειν.
ἐάν
When, whenever, if ever death comes, no one is willing to die.

ὁπότε τινὰς } αἴσθοιτο, ἐπειρᾶτο . . .
εἴ τινας
When, whenever, if ever he saw anyone, he tried . . .

37

(4) A temporal clause may be generic :

χαλεπῶς ἂν τοὺς ἄλλους πείσαιμι, ὅτ. γε μηδ' ὑμᾶς ϳυναμαι πείθειν.
I should have difficulty in persuading the others when I can't even persuade you.

NOTES.—(i) In general temporal clauses the main verb is present or imperfect (not future).

(ii) The rules for subordinate clauses in oratio obliqua apply to temporal clauses.

(iii) The present subjunctive or optative expresses continuous or repeated action.

The aorist subjunctive or optative expresses momentary or single action.

(iv) When dependent on an unfulfilled condition, the clause introduced by ἕως, etc., 'until' takes a historic tense of the indicative (instead of the indefinite construction) :

ἡσυχίαν ἂν ἦγον, ἕως γνώμην ἀπεφήναντο.
I should have waited (but I didn't) until they had declared their opinion.

(v) μέχρι οὗ and other temporal constructions are used by Thucydides with the subjunctive *without* ἄν :

μέχρι οὗ ἐπανέλθωσιν οἱ πρέσβεις.
Until the envoys shall have returned . . .

(vi) Common temporal conjunctions are :

ἐπεί, ἐπειδή, ὡς, 'when, after'.
ὅτε, ὁπότε, ἡνίκα, 'at the time when'.
πρίν, 'before, until' (see below).
ἕως, μέχρι οὗ, ἔστε, 'until'.
ὅσον χρόνον, ἕως, ἔστε, ἐν ᾧ, 'whilst, as long as'.
ὁσάκις, 'as often as'.
ἐπειδὴ τάχιστα, 'as soon as'.
ἐξ οὗ, 'since, from the time when'.

(vii) Note the forms ἐπειδάν, ὅταν, ὁπόταν (ἐπειδὴ + ἄν, etc.).

(viii) ἕως with aorist = 'until', ἕως with present = 'as long as'.

GREEK PROSE USAGE

(ix) (a) ὅτε (ἡνίκα) are relative adverbs and mean 'at the time when':

> Περδίκκας βασιλεὺς ἦν ὅτε Σιτάλκης ἐπῄει.
> Perdiccas was king when Sitalces attacked.

(b) ὅτε marks a date:

> μεμνημένοι ὅτε ἀνεχώρησε.
> Remembering the occasion when he retreated.

(c) ὅτε is used in a causal sense, 'now that'; it is almost equal to ὅτι:

> ὅτε τοίνυν τοῦθ' οὕτως ἔχει, now that this is so ...

(x) ἐπεί, ἐπειδή mean 'now that', 'after' (ἐπειδή is more common). The following sentence shows the difference between ὅτε and ἐπειδή:

> καὶ ἐπειδὴ ἑτοῖμα ἦν, ἐπορεύετο τῇ ὁδῷ ἣν ἐποιήσατο ὅτε ἐπὶ Παίονας ἐστράτευσε.
> And now that all was ready, he set off by the road which he had made when he marched against the Paeonians.

(xi) ὡς is used generally with the aorist, and means rather 'as' than 'when':

> οἱ Πλαταιῆς, ὡς ᾔσθοντο ἔνδον ὄντας τοὺς Θηβαίους, πρὸς ξύμβασιν ἐχώρησαν.
> The Plataeans, becoming aware that the Thebans were inside, came to an arrangement.

With the imperfect:

> οἱ Πελοποννήσιοι, ὡς αἱ μηχαναὶ οὐδὲν ὠφέλουν, παρεσκευάζοντο πρὸς τὴν περιτείχισιν.
> The Peloponnesians, as their machines were of no use, began to prepare for a circumvallation.

(5) 'Before, until' = πρίν.

πρίν with the infinitive or accusative and infintive means 'before'. After a negative πρίν means 'until' and takes the same construction as other temporal conjunctions:

> πολλοὶ ἀπέθανον πρὶν δῆλοι γενέσθαι.
> Many died before it was clear that they ...

πειρώμενοι φθάσαι πρὶν τοὺς πολεμίους καταλαβεῖν τὰ ἄκρα.
Trying to anticipate the enemy's seizing the heights.

οὐ πρόσθεν ἐξενεγκεῖν ἐτόλμησαν πόλεμον πρὶν τοὺς στρατηγοὺς συνέλαβον.
They did not dare to make war until they seized the generals.

οὐ χρή με ἀπελθεῖν πρὶν ἂν δῶ δίκην.
I ought not to depart until I pay the penalty.

ἕκαστον ἔπειθε μὴ πρότερον μηδενὸς ἐπιμελεῖσθαι πρὶν ἑαυτοῦ ἐπιμεληθείη.
He tried to persuade each one not to care for anything until he cared for himself.

NOTES.—(i) πρίν is often preceded by πρότερον or πρόσθεν in the main clause.

(ii) Generally πρίν takes the *aorist* infinitive:

πρὶν ἐσβαίνειν (*present*), before the embarkation began.

(iii) πρὶν ἤ is found for πρίν (probably not in Attic prose). So also πρότερον ἤ, 'before' (for πρότερον πρίν).

(iv) Even after a negative, πρίν may mean 'before' and take the infinitive:

μίαν ἡμέραν οὐκ ἐχήρευσε πρὶν ὡς Ἄφοβον ἐλθεῖν.
She was not a widow a single day before she went to Aphobus.

οὐ πρὶν πάσχειν τοὺς συμμάχους παρεκαλέσατε.
Not previously to your suffering did you summon the allies.

(v) After historic tenses πρὶν ἄν with subjunctive is used only in oratio obliqua (vivid construction):

οὐκ ἔφη ἀπιέναι πρὶν ἂν ἴδῃ τὸν στρατηγόν.
He said he would not go away until he saw the general.

(vi) πρίν with indicative meaning 'until' is sometimes used after an affirmative:

ἐθαύμαζον, πρίν τινες εἶπον.
They wondered, until some said . . .

πρὶν δή, πρίν γε δή, marking the decisive moment:

παραπλήσια δὲ καὶ οἱ ἐπὶ τῶν νεῶν ἔπασχον πρίν γε δὴ οἱ Συρακόσιοι ἔτρεψαν τοὺς Ἀθηναίους.
Those in the ships were suffering much the same, until finally the Syracusans routed the Athenians.

CAUSAL CLAUSES

ὅτι, διότι = 'because'; ἐπεί = 'since' (ἐπείπερ, ἐπειδή); ὡς = 'as'.

The indicative is used, negative οὐ:

ἐπεὶ οὐ θέλετε ἐμοὶ πείθεσθαι, ἐγὼ σὺν ὑμῖν ἕψομαι.
Since you will not obey me, I will follow with you.

οἱ Συρακόσιοι πλείω ἐπορίσαντο ὅτι ἐν μεγίστῳ κινδύνῳ ἦσαν.
The Syracusans furnished more because they were in the greatest danger.

ἦν δὲ ἄξιος ὁ ἀγὼν ὅτι οὐχὶ Ἀθηναίων μόνων περιεγίγνοντο.
The struggle was more worth while, because they were overcoming not only the Athenians.

But in oratio obliqua and virtual oratio obliqua the optative is used for the indicative in the same tense as the oratio recta, except for past tenses in oratio recta, which are not changed. The optative is found only after ὅτι, ὡς, ἐπεί.

In virtual oratio obliqua the alleged reason is given, after verbs of accusing and the like ('on the ground that'):

τὸν Περικλέα ἐκάκιζον ὅτι οὐκ ἐπεξάγοι.
They abused Pericles, because (as they said) he was not leading them out.

NOTES.—(i) διὰ τό with the infinitive is often used for 'because of the fact that'.

(ii) A participle, sometimes with ἅτε or ὡς, may take the place of a causal clause:

τούτων οὕτως ἐχόντων, since this is (was) so.

(iii) The relative pronoun (ὅστις or ὅς γε) with the indicative may express a cause ('in that he . . .'):

κάκιστος ἐνομίζετο ὅστις οὐκ ἀντέστη τοῖς πολεμίοις.

He was considered most cowardly in that he did not resist the enemy.

See also Relative Clauses, p. 55.

(iv) ἐπεί may equal 'for':

> ἐπεὶ τοσόνδε εἰπέ, for tell us this much.

CONCESSIVE CLAUSES

(1) 'Although' = ἐὰν καί, εἰ καί ; 'even if' = καὶ ἐάν (κἄν), καὶ εἰ ; 'not even if' = οὐδ' ἐάν, οὐδ' εἰ.

These conjunctions are followed by the construction of the protasis of a conditional sentence ; negative μή :

καλὸν ἂν ἦν, εἰ καὶ ἡμαρτάνομεν, τοῖσδε εἶξαι.
It would have been honourable for these men to yield, although we were at fault.

καίτοι ταῦτα, καὶ εἰ μικρά τις ἡγεῖται, μεγάλα δείγματά ἐστι.
And yet these are great proofs, even if one thinks them small.

NOTE.—κἂν εἰ (for καὶ ἂν εἰ), 'even if', is used with indicative or optative :

κἂν εἰ πολλαί εἰσιν, ἕν γε εἶδος ἔχουσιν.
Even if they are many, they have one form.

κἂν εἰ τις ἐξαπατηθείη, καλὴ ἡ ἀπάτη.
Even if one were to be deceived, the deceit would be noble.

(2) Usually 'although' is translated by καίπερ with the participle ; negative οὐ (see Uses of the Participles) :

καίπερ εἰδότες.
Although they knew . . .

καίπερ ἐξόν.
Although it is possible.

καίπερ οὐ παρόντος τοῦ στρατηγοῦ.
Although the general was not present.

NOTE.—

καὶ ταῦτα τηλικοῦτος ὤν.
And that, too, though of such an age.

COMPARATIVE CLAUSES

(1) ὅπως, ὡς, ὥσπερ, καθάπερ, mean 'as', often with οὕτω καί in the main clause:

ἐγώ, ὥσπερ ἄλλος τις ἵππῳ ἀγαθῷ ἥδεται, οὕτω καὶ φίλοις ἀγαθοῖς ἥδομαι.

As another man delights in a good horse, so I delight in good friends.

In the *Future*, they are used with ἄν with subjunctive:

τοῦτο ποιήσω ὡς ἄριστα ἂν δύνωμαι.
I shall do it as best I can.

ἡμῖν δοκεῖ διαπορεύεσθαι τὴν χώραν ὡς ἂν δυνώμεθα ἀσινέστατα.
We are determined to march through the land doing as little harm as possible.

In the *Present*, they take the indicative for a definite comparison:

τοῦτο ποιῶ ὡς ἄριστα δύναμαι, I am doing it as best I can.

They take ἄν with subjunctive for a general comparison:

τοῦτο ἀεὶ ποιῶ ὡς ἄριστα ἂν δύνωμαι.
I always do it as best I can.

In the *Past*, they take the indicative for a definite comparison:

τοῦτο ἐποίησα ὡς ἄριστα ἐδυνάμην.
I did it as best I could.

They take the optative for a general comparison:

τοῦτο ἀεὶ ἐποίουν ὡς ἄριστα δυναίμην.
I always used to do it as best I could.

NOTES.—(i)

ὡς πολέμιοι, like enemies.
ὡς, ὅτι τάχιστα, as quickly as possible.
ὡς ἐκ πλείστου, at as great a distance as possible.

(ii) Proportion is expressed by ὅσῳ ... τοσούτῳ:

ὅσῳ πλέον ... τοσούτῳ πλέον, the more ... the more.

ὅσῳπερ means 'exactly in proportion as . . .'.
A double superlative is also used :

οἱ ἰατροὶ μάλιστα ἔθνῃσκον ὅσῳ καὶ μάλιστα προσῇσαν.

The doctors died in greater numbers, as they came more into contact.

(iii) After ἴσος, 'equal', ὁμοῖος, 'like', ὁ αὐτός, 'the same', καί may be used for 'as' :

ἐν ἴσῳ καὶ εἰ μὴ ἐνεθυμήθη . . .

Equally as if he had not thought . . .

Also by the relative :

ταὐτὸν ἔδοξαν ἔχειν ἁμάρτημα ὅπερ καὶ οἱ ποιηταί.

They seemed to have the same error as the poets.

Also by the dative case (*q.v.*). See also Correlatives (p. 49).

(iv) A comparative clause may be attracted into the construction of the main clause :

ἔφη αὐτονόμους τὰς ἐν τῇ Ἀσίᾳ πόλεις εἶναι, ὥσπερ καὶ τὰς ἐν τῇ Ἑλλάδι.

He said that the cities in Asia were autonomous, as those in Greece (are).

(v) Notice the frequent use of καί with a comparison : ὅσῳ καί, ὥσπερ καί, ὅπερ καί. It could be translated 'as also', 'just as'.

(vi) οἷον means 'like', 'for example'. See Correlatives (p. 49).

(vii) οὐχ ὥσπερ comes to mean 'whereas' :

ἔξω τοῦ κακῶς πάσχειν γενήσεσθε, οὐχ ὥσπερ τὸν παρελθόντα χρόνον ᾤχετο ἄγων . . .

You will be out of reach of injury, whereas in time past (Philip) carried off . . .

(2) 'Than' is translated by ἤ, with the same construction as precedes it :

πάντα μᾶλλον ποιήσω ἢ ἀποκρινοῦμαι.

I will do anything rather than answer.

ἤλεγχον εἴ τινα εἰδεῖεν ἄλλην ὁδὸν ἢ τὴν φανεράν.

They questioned whether they knew any other way than the obvious one.

The genitive of comparison is common when the nominative or accusative follows ἤ, less common when the dative follows :

> μείζων ἐστὶ τοῦ ἀδελφοῦ.
> He is taller than his brother.
>
> ὑμῖν αἴσχιον τῶν ἄλλων (ἢ τοῖς ἄλλοις).
> More disgraceful for you than for the others.

It is used with words like ἄλλος, ἕτερος, πρότερος, προτεραῖος, ὕστερος, ὑστεραῖος, διαφέρω, τὸ ἐναντίον, διπλάσιος :

> ὕστεροι τῆς μάχης.
> Too late for the battle.
>
> τῇ ὑστεραίᾳ τῆς μάχης.
> On the day after the battle.
>
> τῇ ὑστεραίᾳ ᾖ ᾗ ἂν ἔλθῃ τὸ πλοῖον, ἀποθανοῦμαι.
> On the day after that of the ship's arrival I shall be executed.

It is found with genitives like ἐλπίδος, λόγου, καιροῦ, γνώμης, τοῦ δέοντος, τοῦ ὄντος (reality) :

> πλέον τοῦ δέοντος, more than necessary.

With πλέον, ἔλαττον, μεῖον, ἤ may be omitted before numbers without affecting the case :

> οὐ μεῖον πεντακοσίους ἀπέκτειναν.
> They killed not less than 500.

But also :

> οὐ μεῖον ἑξήκοντα σταδίων, not less than 60 stades.
> τριήρεις πλέον ἢ εἴκοσιν, more than 20 triremes.
> οὐ μεῖον ἢ μύρια στάδια, not less than 10,000 stades.

But πλείους, ἐλάσσους are found with ἤ or the genitive.

NOTES.—(i) A comparison of two properties of the same subject is expressed by two comparatives :

> ἀνδρειότερος ἢ φρονιμώτερος, more brave than wise.

(ii) Notice the expression

> δυνατώτεροι αὐτοὶ ἑαυτῶν, more powerful than ever.

(iii) The comparative also means 'rather'.

GREEK PROSE USAGE

(iv) The comparative may be used idiomatically for English positive :

οὐδ' ἔστιν οὔτε μεῖζον οὔτ' ἔλαττον ψήφισμα.
There is no decree, great or small.

(v) Comparatio compendiaria — Brachylogy of Comparison :

τούτων (gen. of comparison) τὴν ἐναντίαν ἅπασαν ὁδὸν ἐλήλυθα.
I have come a completely different way from (that of) these men.

(vi) The illogical form of comparison is frequent :

ἀξιολογώτατον τῶν προγεγενημένων.
Literally, Most noteworthy of its predecessors.
i.e. More noteworthy than its predecessors.

(vii) ἀλλὰ ἤ = 'than, except' :

τίνα ἄλλον ἔχουσι λόγον, ἀλλ' ἢ τὸν ὀρθόν τε καὶ δίκαιον;
What other argument have they than the right and just one ?

(viii) πλὴν ἤ (and πλὴν εἰ) used for 'except' (πλήν).

(ix) Pleonastic use of ἤ :

τίς ἂν αἰσχίων εἴη ταύτης δόξα ἢ δοκεῖν;
What reputation could be more disgraceful than this, to be thought . . . ?

(x) Some ways of expressing the superlative :

δυνατὸς εἴ τις ἄλλος
δυνατὸς ὡς οὐδεὶς ἄλλος
πλεῖστα εἰς δυνάμενος } most, very powerful.
οἷος δυνατώτατος
ἐν τοῖς δυνατώτατος

καί ποτε ὄντος πάγου οἵου δεινοτάτου
And when there was once a most terrible frost.

(xi)
ἥδιον ἂν ἀποθάνοιμι ἢ παραδοίην τὰ ὅπλα.
I would sooner die than hand over my arms.

The second clause does not take ἄν.

(xii) A comparative means 'too':

> μεῖζον ἢ κατὰ δάκρυα.
> Too great for tears.
>
> ἐνδεεστέρως ἢ πρὸς τὴν ἐξουσίαν }
> ἐνδεεστέρως παρὰ τὴν ἐξουσίαν }
> Too sparingly for their means.
>
> μεῖζον ἢ φέρειν.
> Too great to bear (to be borne).

This is more usually μεῖζον ἢ ὥστε (ὡς) φέρειν.

(3) 'Than if', ἢ εἰ; 'as if', ὥσπερ εἰ (ὡσπερεί), οἷον εἰ; 'as though', ὥσπερ ἂν εἰ (ὡσπερανεί), οἷόνπερ.

These take the construction of the protasis of unreal conditions: with the optative, 'as if one were to do'; with imperfect indicative, 'as if one were doing'; with aorist indicative, 'as if one did (had done)':

> οὐδὲν διάφορον πάσχει ἢ εἰ ἐστρατεύετο.
> He is treated exactly as if he were a soldier.

The participle can be used, ὤν being frequently omitted:

> ὡσπερανεὶ παῖς (ὤν), like a child.
> ὥσπερ ἂν εἰ ἡγούμενοι, as though thinking.
> οἷόνπερ ὑμνοῦντες, as though singing.

CORRELATIVES

DEMONSTRATIVES have corresponding relatives; where in English this relative is 'as', in Greek the relative corresponding to the demonstrative is used:

οὕτω(ς), so	ὡς, as
τοιοῦτος, of such a sort	οἷος, as
τοσοῦτος, of such a size	ὅσος, as
τοσοῦτοι, as many	ὅσοι, as
ὁ αὐτός, the same	{ ὅσπερ / καί / the dative } as
οὗτος, this man	ὅς, ὅστις, who
ἐκεῖ, there	οὗ, where
ἐκεῖσε, thither	οἷ, whither
ἐκεῖθεν, thence	ὅθεν, whence
τότε, then	ὅτε, when

Examples:

ὑμεῖς τοσοῦτοι ὄντες ὅσοι νῦν συνεληλύθατε.
You being so many as are now assembled.

τοσοῦτόν σε ἐγίνωσκον ὅσον ἤκουον Ἀθηναῖον εἶναι.
I had taken so much notice of you, as I heard you were an Athenian.

NOTES.—(i) The agreement of the relative is as in Relative Clauses (*q.v.*).

(ii) The relative clause often precedes the main clause and the demonstrative is used in the main clause though usually omitted in English.

(iii) Notice the expression:

οἷος σὺ ἀνήρ, such a man as you.

All three words are declined together.

(iv) For οἷος with infinitive see Consecutive Clauses,

but remember the difference between 'such . . . as' and 'such . . . as to (that)'.

(v) οἷον means 'for example', 'like':

> εἰ δ' αὖ οἷον ἀποδομῆσαί ἐστιν ὁ θάνατος ἐνθένδε.
> But if death is like leaving this place.

(vi) ὅσον means 'about':

> ὅσον ὀκτὼ σταδίους, about 8 stades (a mile).

RELATIVE CLAUSES

A. DEFINITE

When the relative refers to a definite person or thing (or time, place, manner), it takes the indicative (negative οὐ), or any other construction which would occur in an independent sentence:

ὃ μὴ γένοιτο.
May it not happen!

τῶν Ἀθηναίων πρέσβεις, οἳ ἔτυχον παρόντες.
Ambassadors of the Athenians, who happened to be present.

NOTES.—(i) ἔνθα, 'where', ἔνθεν, 'whence', are relatives in prose, except in the phrases ἔνθα καὶ ἔνθα, 'here and there', ἔνθεν καὶ ἔνθεν, 'on both sides (on one side and on the other)' and in Xenophon ἔνθα δή, 'then indeed'.

(ii) ἦ δ' ὅς, 'said he'; ἦ δ' ὃς ὁ Σωκράτης, 'said Socrates'; καὶ ὅς, 'and he'; ὃς δ' ἔφη, 'said he'.

(iii) ὃς μέν ... ὃς δέ used in oblique cases for ὁ μέν ... ὁ δέ, 'one ... another':

πόλεις Ἑλληνίδας ἃς μὲν ἀναιρῶν, εἰς ἃς δὲ κατάγων τοὺς φυγάδας.
Destroying some Hellenic cities, to others restoring the exiles.

(iv) ἔστιν οἵ (οὕς, ὧν, οἷς) or εἰσὶν οἵ = 'some'. The imperfect is usually ἦσαν οἵ:

ἔστιν ἐν οἷς, in some things.

(v)
οὐκ ἔσθ' ὅπως, impossible.
οὐκ ἔσθ' ὅπως οὐ, undoubtedly.
ἔστιν ὅτε, sometimes.

(vi)
οὐδεὶς ὅστις οὔ, everybody.

This phrase is treated as one word, *e.g.* accusative is:

> οὐδένα ὅντινα οὐ κατέκλασε τῶν παρόντων.
> He broke down all of those present.

(vii)

> ὅτου δὴ παρεγγυήσαντος.
> Someone or other passing the word.

(viii)

> μετὰ ἱδρῶτος θαυμαστοῦ ὅσου.
> With a wonderful amount of sweat.
>
> θαυμαστῶς ὡς, wonderfully.
> ὡς ἀληθῶς, in truth.
> ὡς ἑτέρως, amiss.

(ix)

> ὅσαι ἡμέραι (ὁσημέραι), daily.

(x) A preposition is usually omitted with the relative, when it has been used with the antecedent:

> ἐν τῷ πλοίῳ ᾧ, in the ship in which.

(xi) The relative is often not repeated, though in a different case:

> οἷς μέλει . . . ἀλλὰ ζῶσιν, who care for . . . but live.

The demonstrative is usually put for the repeated relative, if in an oblique case:

> ὅσοι εἰργασμένοι εἰσίν, ὀφείλεται δ' αὐτοῖς.
> Those who have done . . . and to whom there is due.

But the relative is repeated if the first clause is negative and the second affirmative:

> οὐκ ἐν ᾧ κεῖνται μᾶλλον ἀλλ' ἐν ᾧ ἡ δόξα καταλείπεται.
> Not the tomb in which they lie but rather that in which their glory is left behind.

(xii) The negative μή is found with a definite relative when it expresses a cause or result conceived as ideal rather than real:

> οἷς μηδὲ ἐπελθεῖν οἷόν τε ἦν.
> Inasmuch as it was impossible even to get at them.

Agreement of Relative Pronoun

It takes its number, gender, person from its antecedent but its case from its own clause.

> τοὺς ἐμπόρους, οἳ ἔτυχον παρόντες, ἀπέκτειναν.
> They killed the merchants who happened to be present.

NOTE.—When the relative clause contains a predicative noun, the relative agrees

(a) with the antecedent, when the clause is necessary to complete the sense:

> τὸ μέγιστον νόσημα ὃ στάσις καλεῖται.
> That serious disease called faction.

(b) with the predicative noun, when the clause is not essential:

> φίλος, ὃ μέγιστον ἀγαθὸν εἶναί φασιν.
> A friend, the greatest blessing, they say.

Relative Attraction

(a) The relative, when *object*, is attracted to the case of its antecedent, when genitive or dative: τῶν δώρων ὧν for τῶν δώρων ἅ. So when the antecedent is drawn into the relative clause: αἷς ἔλαβον ναυσίν for ταῖς ναυσὶν ἃς ἔλαβον.

NOTES.—(i) ὅστις is never attracted, but ὅσος, οἷος and ἡλίκος are attracted like ὅς.

(ii) Attraction does not occur when the relative is connective:

> πάντων ὧν εἶχον ἀγαθῶν σοι μετέδωκα, ἃ σὺ φαυλίζεις.
> I gave you a share of all the good things I had, and you despise them.

(b) (i) A demonstrative antecedent is often omitted when the relative would be in the accusative: περὶ ὧν for περὶ τούτων οὕς (or ἅ).

> σὺν οἷς μάλιστα φιλεῖς (σὺν ἐκείνοις οὕς).
> With those whom you like most.

(ii) A demonstrative as antecedent may be omitted in the nominative or accusative :

οἷς τὰ παρόντα ἀρκεῖ, οὐκ ὀρέγονται.
Those, for whom the present is enough, do not seek . . .

ἐὰν ἐμοὶ ὧν δέομαι ὑπηρετήσητε (ταῦτα ὧν . . .).
If you supply me with what I need.

(iii) The relative may be attracted into the case of an omitted antecedent, with agreement of predicative adjective in the relative clause :

ὧν ἔκρινα δικαίων οὐδὲν προδοῦναι (τούτων ἃ ἔκρινα δίκαια).
Not to betray any of the things I considered just.

(c) (i) The antecedent may be attracted into the case of the relative and drawn into the relative clause :

ὧν ἀπείχοντο κερδῶν αἰσχρὰ νομίζοντες.
Counting disgraceful the profits from which they abstained.

Note the omission of the article.

(ii) The antecedent may be attracted into the case of the relative, but not drawn into the relative clause :

ἔλεγον ὅτι πάντων ὧν δέονται ἔπραξαν (πάντα ὧν).
They said they had done all the things they needed.

Other uses of the relative :

(i) ὅστις with the future indicative (negative μή) expresses a purpose in primary or historic time.

ξυνέδρους ἑλέσθαι ἐκέλευον οἵτινες ξυμβήσονται.
They bade them choose councillors to come to an agreement.

The potential ἄν with optative is also used (for the future indicative) :

ἡνίκ᾽ ἂν ἡμεῖς μὴ δυναίμεθα ἀφικέσθαι . . .
In order that we should not then reach . . .

In past time we find :

χειροτονεῖν ἐβούλεσθε ἐξ ὧν τὰ πράγματα ἤμελλεν ὡς φαυλότατα ἕξειν.
You wished to pass measures for the utter ruining of the state.

(ii) ὅστις or ὅς γε with the indicative (negative οὐ or μή) expresses a cause ('since, in that'):

οἵ γε μηδὲ ἀπὸ πολιτειῶν τοιούτων ἥκετε.
Since also you do not come from such states.

(iii) ὅστις or ὅς with the indicative, or ἄν with the optative (negative οὐ) expresses a result, usually after negatives:

οὐδεὶς ἂν γένοιτο οὕτως ἀδαμάντινος ὃς ἂν μείνειε.
No one would be so unmoved that he would remain firm.

(iv) ὅς is used for the demonstrative:

καὶ ὃς ἀκούσας . . ., and he, hearing . . .

(v) Connective relative:

οὗ δὴ ὄντα τὸν Σιτάλκην οἱ Ἀθηναῖοι ξύμμαχον ἐποιήσαντο.
His son, then, Sitalces the Athenians made an ally.

B. INDEFINITE

A relative clause with an indefinite antecedent has a conditional force. Negative μή.

(1) *Present*

(*a*) Particular: indicative in both clauses:

ἃ μὴ οἶδα } οὐδὲ οἴομαι εἰδέναι.
εἴ τινα μὴ οἶδα }

What I do not know   } I do not (now) think I
If there is anything I do not know } know.

This use is also called generic — the sort of thing I do not know. The specific case can always be put generically.

(*b*) General (denoting repetition or indefinite frequency): Relative with ἄν and the subjunctive; indicative main clause:

συμμαχεῖν τούτοις ἐθέλουσι πάντες, οὓς ἂν ὁρῶσι παρεσκευασμένους (ἐάν τινας ὁρῶσι).
All men are (always) willing to join those whom (whomsoever) they see ready.

GREEK PROSE USAGE

(c) **Unfulfilled**: relative clause imperfect indicative; main clause ἄν with imperfect indicative:

οὐκ ἂν ἐπεχειροῦμεν πράττειν $\begin{Bmatrix} ἅ \\ εἴ τινα \end{Bmatrix}$ μὴ ἠπιστάμεθα.

We should not be undertaking (as we are) to do what we did not understand.

(2) *Past*

(a) **Particular**: indicative in both clauses:

$\begin{Bmatrix} οὕς \\ εἴ τινας \end{Bmatrix}$ μὴ εὕρισκον, κενοτάφιον αὐτοῖς ἐποίησαν.

They made a cenotaph for any whom (such as) they did not find.

ἐπανηρώτων τὸν Σωκράτη ὃ μὴ ἐμεμνήμην.

I used to ask Socrates anything I did not remember.

(b) **General** (indefinite frequency): relative clause in optative; main clause indicative:

$\begin{Bmatrix} ἐπειδή \\ εἴ ποτε \end{Bmatrix}$ ἀνοιχθείη, εἰσῇμεν.

We used to go in, whenever the prison was opened.

ὁπόσον προδιώξειαν, τοσοῦτον πάλιν ἐπαναχωρεῖν ἔδει.

As far as they advanced in pursuit, so far they had to retire.

(c) **Unfulfilled**: relative clause in past indicative; main clause ἄν with aorist indicative:

$\begin{Bmatrix} ἅ \\ εἴ τινα \end{Bmatrix}$ μὴ ἐβούλετο δοῦναι, οὐκ ἂν ἔδωκεν.

He would not have given what he did not wish to give.

(3) *Future*

(a) **Open**: relative clause with ἄν and subjunctive; main clause future indicative:

$\begin{Bmatrix} ὅ, τι ἂν \\ ἐάν τι \end{Bmatrix}$ βούληται, δώσω.

I will give him whatever he wants.

(b) **Vague**: relative clause with optative, main clause with ἄν and optative.

$\begin{Bmatrix} ὅ, τι \\ εἴ τι \end{Bmatrix}$ βούλοιτο, δοίην ἄν.

I should give him whatever he wished.

IMPERSONAL VERBS

(1) THOSE denoting weather and natural phenomena, *e.g.* ὕει, 'it rains', ἔσεισε, 'there was an earthquake'.

(2) δεῖ, χρή, 'must, ought', take the accusative and infinitive. Note:

> τί ἔδει, ἐχρῆν (χρῆν) με ποιεῖν;
> What was I to do? What ought I to have done?

(3) Those like ἔξεστι, 'it is possible', δοκεῖ, 'it seems good', taking the dative and the infinitive:

> ἔδοξεν αὐτοῖς ἀπελθεῖν, they decided to go away.

(4) μέλει, 'it is a care', takes the dative of the person and the genitive of the noun or the dative and the infinitive. It may have τοῦτο, ταῦτα (neuter pronouns) as subject:

> μέλει μοι ταῦτα, these things are a care to me.
> οὐδέν μοι μέλει τῆς ἀρετῆς, I care not for virtue.

μεταμέλει, 'it repents', takes the dative of the person and the genitive of the noun, or a participle agreeing with the dative of the person:

> μεταμέλει μοι ταῦτα ποιήσαντι.
> I repent of having done these things.

(5) Passive verbs of saying, *e.g.* λέγεται, 'it is said', εἴρηται, 'it has been said' (also used personally: see Oratio Obliqua), and the perfect and pluperfect passive of other verbs are used impersonally (with the dative of the agent), *e.g.*:

> ἡμῖν παρεσκεύασται, preparations have been made by us.
> ὡς εἴρηται, as has been said (ordered).

(6) Verbs like σημαίνει, 'the signal is given', ἐκήρυξε,

'a proclamation was made', where the real subject is understood (*i.e.* the herald, the trumpeter):

> ὡς ἐσήμηνε τοῖς Ἕλλησιν.
> When the signal was given to the Greeks.

NOTES.—(i) φανερός, δῆλος, δίκαιος ('I am clear, right') are used personally:

> δῆλοί εἰσιν οὐ μένοντες.
> It is clear that they are not staying.
>
> δίκαιός εἰμι ἀπολογήσασθαι.
> It is right for me to defend myself.

We also find δίκαιόν ἐστι with the accusative and infinitive, and δικαίως ἄν with optative ('I should be justified'). So also ἔοικα, 'I seem':

> ἔοικεν οὐ πατὴρ εἶναι, it seems he is not a father.

But also ὡς ἔοικεν, 'as it seems'.

(Note δῆλον ὅτι (as one word), 'obviously' (lit. 'it is clear that').

(ii) δοκεῖ μοι, 'it seems good to me (I decide)'.

(iii) The negative with impersonal verbs is οὐ, *e.g.* οὐ δεῖ; but an infinitive after an impersonal verb takes μή:

> ἡμᾶς δεῖ μήποτε ἐξαπατηθῆναι ὑπὸ τούτων.
> We must never be deceived by these men.
>
> ὧν προλυπηθῆναι δεῖ ἢ μηδὲ ἡσθῆναι.
> (Pleasures) from which one must receive pain first or not enjoy at all.

(iv) The participles of impersonal verbs are used absolutely in the accusative, *e.g.* δέον, 'it being necessary', δόξαν, 'it having been decided'. But with verbs denoting weather the genitive is used: ὕοντος, 'as it was raining'.

THE USES OF THE PARTICIPLES

(1) THE article with the participle is equivalent to a relative clause.
   (a) Definite : οἱ οὐ βουλόμενοι, 'those who did not wish'.
   (b) Indefinite : οἱ μὴ βουλόμενοι, 'any who do not wish'.

(2) ὡς with the future participle expresses purpose : ὡς is omitted with verbs of motion. Negative οὐ :

προσβολὰς παρεσκευάζοντο ὡς ποιησόμενοι.
They made preparations with a view to making attacks.

ἔπεμψαν ἡμᾶς πράξοντας περὶ τῶν ἐν τῇ νήσῳ.
They sent us to make arrangements about those on the island.

The article is frequently used with this participle :

ὁ ἡγησόμενος οὐδεὶς ἔσται, there will be no one to lead us.

(3) The participle is used for a temporal clause :

ἐκέλευσεν αὐτὸν διαβάντα τὴν θάλασσαν ἔπειτα ἀπαλλάττεσθαι.
He ordered him to withdraw only after he had crossed the sea.

Note ἔπειτα (or τότε), 'only after, not until'.

εὐθύς, παραυτίκα with a participle mean 'as soon as' :

εὐθὺς ἀποβεβηκότες, immediately after landing.

ἅμα, μεταξύ with a participle mean 'in the act of, in the middle of, while' :

ἅμα προϊὼν ἐπεσκοπεῖτο.
As he went on, he considered . . .

πολλαχοῦ δή με ἐπέσχε λέγοντα μεταξύ.
It often checked me in the middle of speaking.

ἄρτι with past participle means 'soon after' :

ἄρτι τῆς μάχης γεγενημένης.
Soon after the battle had taken place.

(4) καίπερ with a participle means 'although'. Negative οὐ:

καίπερ οὐκ εἰδότες, although they did not know . . .

(5) ἅτε, οἷον, οἷα δή with participle mean 'because, inasmuch as'. Negative οὐ:

ἅτε νομίζων ἀμείνονας εἶναι ὑμᾶς προσέλαβον.
I took you with me, as I thought you better.

(6) ὡς with participle expresses a thought or supposition, 'on the ground that, thinking that'. Negative οὐ:

ἔτι δὲ δόξω ἀμελῆσαι, ὡς οἷός τε ὢν σε σῴζειν.
I shall be thought negligent, on the ground that I am able to save you.

(7) A participle may stand for the protasis of a condition. The tense used is that of the finite verb represented by the participle (present for present and imperfect), but not the future. Negative μή:

μηδὲν αἰσχρὸν ποιοῦντες.
If you do nothing dishonourable.

μὴ κατηγορήσαντος Αἰσχίνου μηδέν, οὐδ' ἂν ἐγὼ λόγον οὐδέν' ἐποιούμην ἕτερον.
If Aeschines had made no accusation, I should not now be adding any different argument.

(8) ὥσπερ with participle means 'as it were, as if'. Negative οὐ:

ὥσπερ οὐκ ἐπὶ σοὶ ὄν, as if it were not in your power.

See Comparative Clauses (3).

(9) Many participles are used with adverbial force, e.g.:

ἀρχόμενος, at first.
φθάσας, sooner.
ἀνύσας, quickly.
θαρρῶν, cheerfully.
συνελών, briefly.

τελευτῶν, at last.
λαθών, secretly.
χαίρων, with impunity.
παίζων, in jest, for fun.
τί βουλόμενος; with what purpose?

δέον, ἐξόν (with infinitive), instead of (though you might).
τί μαθών, what induces (induced) you to . . . ?
τί παθών, what possesses (possessed) you to . . . ?

Examples :

τοῖς ἱππεῦσιν εἴρητο θαρροῦσι διώκειν.
Orders had been given to the cavalry to pursue with confidence.

τί τοῦτο μαθὼν προσέγραψεν;
What induced him to add *this* clause ?

(10) The participle is used as the complement (instead of the infinitive) after many verbs, such as :

ἀνέχομαι, suffer, endure.
ἀγανακτέω, ἄχθομαι, be annoyed.
αἰσχύνομαι, be ashamed.
ἄρχω, begin.
διατελέω, continue.
δῆλός εἰμι, be clear.
ἐλλείπω, fail.
ἥδομαι, be glad.
θαμίζω, be accustomed.
καρτερέω, persevere.
κάμνω, be weary.
λήγω, cease.

λανθάνω, escape notice.
μεταμέλομαι, repent.
παύω, stop.
παύομαι, cease.
περιοράω, allow.
τυγχάνω, happen.
χαλεπῶς φέρω, be annoyed.
φθάνω, anticipate.
φαίνομαι, seem.
φανερός εἰμι, be clear.
χαίρω, rejoice.

NOTE.—λανθάνω, φθάνω, τυγχάνω are used with the aorist participle. See also pp. 62, 64, 125.

ἔλαθεν ἐλθών.
He came secretly.

λήσετε τῆς πολιτείας παραχωρήσαντες.
You will insensibly surrender the constitution.

αἱ νῆες φθάνουσιν αὐτοὺς προκαταφυγοῦσαι.
The ships get away before them.

(11) The Genitive Absolute : (a) A noun or pronoun and a participle in agreement in the genitive case form the genitive absolute and are equivalent to adverbial clauses of many kinds, *e.g.* temporal, conditional, concessive, causal.

The particle ὡς is often added to mean 'because' καίπερ, 'although', ὥσπερ, 'as if'.

The noun or pronoun in this case is not grammatically connected with the main construction of the sentence:

Κόνωνος στρατηγοῦντος { as / when / since / if } Conon was general.

NOTE.—The noun or pronoun is sometimes omitted, when it can be easily supplied from the context or is a general word like ἀνθρώπων or πραγμάτων:

οὕτως ἐχόντων, this being so.

(b) With Impersonal Verbs (q.v.) the accusative absolute is used:

ἐξόν, it being possible.
δέον, it being necessary.

So also with passive verbs used impersonally:

εἰρημένον, when it has been said.

And the participle ὄν:

ἀδύνατον ὄν, it being impossible.

But with impersonal verbs of weather the genitive is used:

ὕοντος πολλῷ, when it was raining heavily.

NOTES.—(i) τυχόν (neuter aorist participle of τυγχάνω) is used as an adverb = 'perhaps'.

(ii) δόξαν ταῦτα or δόξαντα ταῦτα is found, meaning 'this being decided'.

(iii) An accusative absolute is used with ὡς or ὥσπερ in apposition to a sentence meaning 'in the belief that, considering that':

μισθὸν αἰτοῦσιν, ὡς οὐχὶ αὐτοῖσιν ὠφελίαν ἐσομένην.
They demand pay, considering that it is not they who will benefit.

NOTES ON PARTICIPLES.—(i) λανθάνω and φθάνω are

used in the aorist participle to mean 'secretly' and 'sooner, first':

> ἦλθε λαθών, he came secretly.

(ii) φαίνομαι with infinitive, 'I seem to . . .'.
   φαίνομαι with participle ⎫
   φανερός εἰμι   ,,   ⎬ 'I evidently am'.
   δῆλός εἰμι   ,,   ⎭
φανερόν, δῆλόν ἐστι, 'it is plain', are used with a ὅτι clause.

(iii) ἄρχω, ἄρχομαι, 'begin', have infinitive or participle:

> ἡ νόσος (πρῶτον) ἤρξατο γενέσθαι, the plague began to happen.

ἄρχω (often with πρῶτος) with genitive or infinitive frequently means 'I am first to, I make a beginning of':

> ἀγωνίσασθε τοῖς Ἕλλησι ἄρξαι πρῶτοι ἐλευθερίας.
> Strive to begin the work of liberation for the Greeks.

(iv)
> αἰσχύνομαι λέγων, I am ashamed to say (lit. saying).
> αἰσχύνομαι λέγειν, I am prevented by shame from saying.

(v) With λυσιτελεῖ, συμφέρει, μεταμέλει, the participle is used in agreement with the indirect object:

> μεταμέλει μοι ποιήσαντι (for ποιῆσαι).
> I repent of having done it.

(vi)
> οὐκ ἂν φθάνοις λέγων, tell me at once,

'expressing that which, when it takes place, will not take place too soon' (Madvig).

(vii) The negative with participles is οὐ, except when the participle equals an indefinite relative clause or the protasis of a condition. See The Negative.

(viii) The participles βουλόμενος, ἡδόμενος, προσδεχόμενος are used in agreement with a dative depending on ἐστί, γίγνεται (Dative of Reference):

> βουλομένῳ ἐστὶ τῷ πλήθει, the multitude is inclined.

(ix) For the participle in indirect speech see Oratio Obliqua.

(x) The participle is used predicatively:

> ἅμα τῷ σίτῳ ἀκμάζοντι.
> At the time of the ripening of the corn.

And so in other expressions of time with μετά, ἐπί, ἅμα. Also:

> διὰ τούτους οὐ πεισθέντας.
> Owing to these men's non-compliance.
>
> τὸ χωρίον κτιζόμενον.
> The founding of the place.

(xi) The present (or perfect) participle is used to express continuous time, like the present and imperfect indicative (see The Verb: Tenses). With ἤδη in primary time or τότε in historic time, it refers to a completed period past at the time of speaking. With ἔτι it refers to the completion of a period in the future:

> ἐπὶ Χρυσίδος τότε ἱερωμένης πεντήκοντα ἔτη.
> When Chrysis had then been priestess for 50 years.
>
> πόλις ἑπτακόσια ἔτη ἤδη οἰκουμένη.
> A city which has been inhabited now for 700 years.
>
> Πυθοδώρου ἔτι τέσσαρας μῆνας ἄρχοντος.
> When Pythodorus had still four months of office to run.

(xii) The perfect participle is used with τυγχάνω, λανθάνω, φθάνω for a completed action:

> αἱ θύραι ἀνεῳγμέναι ἔτυχον, the gates happened to be open.

The aorist participle denotes time coincident with the verb:

> ἔτυχεν ἐλθών, he happened to come (by chance he came).

But:

> ἔτυχον αὐλιζόμενοι (*imperfect participle*).
> They were camping by chance.
>
> ἐτύγχανον λέγων.
> I happened to be saying.

(xiii) When a participle and a finite verb have a common object, that object follows the construction of the participle:

> ἐς Ἐλευσῖνα ἐσβαλόντες ἐδῄωσαν.
> They invaded and ravaged Eleusis.

(xiv) περιοράω is used with infinitive (in Thucydides) when it equals ἐάω:

> ἤλπιζεν τοὺς Ἀθηναίους τὴν γῆν οὐκ ἂν περιϊδεῖν τμηθῆναι.
> He expected that the Athenians would not let their land be ravaged.

(xv) The participle of the potential (ἄν with participle):

> ὡς τῶν γε παρόντων οὐκ ἂν πράξαντες χεῖρον.
> Since their plight could not be worse than it is.

See Further Notes on Conditional Sentences (p. 31).

(xvi)

> καὶ ταῦτα ἀρνούμενος τὴν χρείαν.
> And that too though he denied the connexion.

(xvii) The participle often contains a more important idea than that of the main verb:

> οὐδὲν τῶν δεόντων ποιούντων ὑμῶν κακῶς τὰ πράγματ' ἔχει.
> The evil plight of your affairs is due to your neglect of duty.

> φυλάξας τὸν χειμῶνα ἐπιχειρεῖ.
> He waits for the winter to commence operations.

(xviii) The participle may express the means by which the action of the main verb is brought about:

> τὰς προφάσεις δεῖ ὑμᾶς ἀφελεῖν, μισθὸν πορίσαντας.
> You must remove their excuses by supplying pay.

(xix) ὅσα μή with the participle means 'except in so much as, provided only . . . not':

> φυλάσσειν τὴν νῆσον Ἀθηναίους, ὅσα μὴ ἀποβαίνοντας.
> The Athenians should guard the island, provided only they did not land.

THE USES OF THE INFINITIVE

(1) THE INFINITIVE AS SUBJECT OR PREDICATE.—The article is used when the infinitive is the true subject:

> τοῦτό ἐστι τὸ ἀδικεῖν, injustice is this.

No article is used when it is predicate or completes the predicate:

> τοῦτο μανθάνειν καλεῖται.
> This is called learning.
>
> οὐχ ἡδὺ πολλοὺς ἐχθροὺς ἔχειν.
> It is not pleasant to have many enemies.

NOTE.—The subject of the infinitive is understood to be 3rd person:

> δοκεῖν γὰρ εἰδέναι ἐστίν, ἃ οὐκ οἶδεν.
> For it is to seem to know what one does not know.

(2) PROLATIVE INFINITIVE.—(*a*) Many verbs (as in English) have an infinitive to complete their meaning. But see The Uses of the Participles for verbs taking a participle instead of an infinitive.

(*b*) Verbs followed by an indirect command have the infinitive. See Indirect Commands.

(*c*) Verbs of hoping, promising, swearing take future infinitive. See Indirect Statements.

(*d*) ἀγγέλλω (παραγγέλλω) with dative and infinitive means 'I send word'.

(*e*) κινδυνεύω with the infinitive is used to translate 'perhaps'.

> κινδυνεύω πεπονθέναι, perhaps I have experienced . . .

(*f*) μέλλω is used with present or future infinitive, rarely with aorist.

GREEK PROSE USAGE

(*g*) ἔχω and infinitive means 'I am able':

> εἴ τις ἔχει πόρους ἑτέρους λέγειν . . .
> If anyone can mention other revenues.

(3) INFINITIVE OF PURPOSE.—This is used with verbs of electing, appointing, giving, offering and the like:

> τὴν βουλὴν ἐπέστησαν ἐπιμελεῖσθαι . . .
> They appointed the council to take charge of . . .
>
> τὴν πόλιν φυλάττειν τοῖς Λακεδαιμονίοις παρέδωκαν.
> They gave the city to the Lacedaemonians to guard.

NOTES.—(i) This infinitive is not used in the passive:

> παρέχει ἑαυτὸν ἐρωτᾶν, he offers himself to be questioned.

(ii) Verbs of bringing, sending, leaving behind usually have the future participle to express the purpose.

(4) INFINITIVE WITH ADJECTIVES (epexegetic, limiting).—(*a*) Many adjectives like ἱκανός, δυνατός, ἑτοῖμος, πρόθυμος, δεινός, ἄξιος take the infinitive, active or passive:

> ἄξιος θαυμάζεσθαι or θαυμάζειν, worthy to be admired.

NOTES.—(i) Sometimes ὥστε is used:

> ὀλίγοι ὥστε, (too) few to . . .

(ii) δίκαιός εἰμι with the infinitive means 'I have a right, I deserve, it is right for me'.

(*b*) Adjectives meaning 'easy, hard, beautiful, pleasant', like χαλεπός, καλός, ἡδύς, take the infinitive:

> καλὸς ἰδεῖν, beautiful to see.

(*c*) After a comparative with ἤ, more usually with ὥστε or ὡς:

> μεῖζον ἢ φέρειν, too great to bear.

(5) INFINITIVE OF LIMITATION OR ABSOLUTE INFINITIVE, *e.g.*—

(*a*)

πολλοῦ δεῖν, far from it.
ὀλίγου δεῖν, almost.
δοκεῖν μοι, in my opinion.

τὸ νῦν εἶναι, at present.
σχεδὸν εἰπεῖν, almost.

(b) With ὡς or ὥς γε :

ὡς ἐπὶ πᾶν εἰπεῖν.
To speak generally.

ὡς (ἔπος) εἰπεῖν.
So to speak (not apologizing for a metaphor, but limiting a sweeping or universal statement), e.g. :

οὐδὲν ἐπιστάμενος, ὡς ἔπος εἰπεῖν.
Knowing practically nothing.

(ὡς) συνελόντι εἰπεῖν.
To speak concisely.

(The participle συνελών means 'briefly').

ὡς ὑπομνῆσαι, as a reminder.

(c) With ὅσον or ὅσα :

ὅσον γ' ἐμὲ εἰδέναι, as far as I know.

(d) ἑκὼν εἶναι, 'deliberately', after a negative :

οὐκ ᾤμην ὑπὸ σοῦ ἑκόντος εἶναι ἐξαπατᾶσθαι.
I did not think to be deceived by you, at least deliberately.

νομίζων οὐ τὸ ὑπομένειν ἑκόντας εἶναι καὶ μάχεσθαι σωτηρίαν.
Considering that safety lay not in their remaining and fighting, unless obliged . . .

(6) THE INFINITIVE WITH THE ARTICLE.—(a) Used as subject :

χαλεπὸν τὸ μετρίως εἰπεῖν.
To speak with moderation is difficult.

(b) Used as object, very occasionally :

φοβούμενοι τὸ καταπεσεῖν.
Being afraid of falling down.

τὸ ἀμύνεσθαι κάλλιον ἡγησάμενοι . . .
Thinking resistance nobler.

(c) In accusative after prepositions, e.g. διά, ἐπί, πρός, εἰς, κατά, παρά :

διὰ τὸ ξυνδιαιτᾶσθαι, through being domesticated.

(d) In genitive, as object of verbs, nouns, adjectives, adverbs and prepositions, e.g. ἀντί, ἕνεκα, πλήν, περί, ἐκ :

τὸ ἀφανὲς τοῦ κατορθώσειν, the uncertainty of success.
ἐκ τοῦ μὴ ἐρημοῦσθαι, as a result of not being depopulated.

NOTES.—(i) Phrases like ἐξουσίαν διδόναι, πρόφασιν παρέχειν usually take the simple infinitive ; so do verbs like ἐπιθυμέω, μέμνημαι, ἐπιλανθάνομαι.

(ii) Verbs of hindering and preventing (q.v.) can take τοῦ with the infinitive.

(e) In the dative (i) of cause, (ii) after a preposition :

τῷ ἐμπειρότεροι εἶναι, through being more experienced.
ἐν τῷ ζῆν ἔτι, in living longer.

(7) THE ARTICLE WITH THE ACCUSATIVE AND INFINITIVE = 'the fact that'.—(a) As subject :

τὸ χρόνον πολὺν γεγενῆσθαι λήθην τινὰ ἐμπεποίηκεν ὑμῖν.
The fact that much time has elapsed has implanted some forgetfulness in you.

(b) As object of a verb or preposition, e.g. διά :

διὰ τὸ εἰωθέναι τοὺς πολλοὺς διαιτᾶσθαι.
On account of the fact that the majority were accustomed to live . . .

(c) In apposition to a noun or pronoun :

τόδε μοι δοκεῖ εὖ λέγεσθαι, τὸ θεοὺς εἶναι.
This, namely that there are gods, seems to me well said.

Also expressed by a ὅτι clause :

τὰ μὲν ἄλλα ὀρθῶς ἤκουσας, ὅτι δὲ οἴει . . . παρήκουσας.
The rest you heard aright, but as to your thinking . . . you misheard.

(d) In dative = by reason of.
Also used with adjectives and prepositions :

ταῦτ' ἔπραξεν Φίλιππος τῷ δικαιότερα ἀξιοῦν τοὺς Θηβαίους.
Philip did this by reason of the fact that the Thebans made more just demands.

(e) In genitive, as for simple infinitive with article:

ὁ ὑπὲρ τοῦ ταῦτα μὴ γενέσθαι ἀγών.
The contest for the prevention of these things from happening.

A genitive of purpose is found, generally negative (rare except in Thucydides):

τοῦ μὴ λῃστὰς κακουργεῖν, to prevent pirates from ravaging.

(8) THE INFINITIVE IN INDIRECT STATEMENT (*q.v.*).
(9) THE INFINITIVE IN INDIRECT COMMAND (*q.v.*).
(10) THE INFINITIVE IN CONSECUTIVE CLAUSES (*q.v.*).
(11) THE INFINITIVE WITH πρίν (*q.v.*).
(12) THE INFINITIVE OF EXCLAMATION (often with the article):

τὸ Δία νομίζειν, to believe in Zeus!

For the tenses of the infinitive see The Verb.

THE ADJECTIVE

(1) THE *Attributive Adjective* stands between the article and the noun or after the noun with the article repeated :

ὁ σοφὸς ἀνήρ or ὁ ἀνὴρ ὁ σοφός, the wise man.

The second form is the rarer, chiefly used for a 'nearer specification' of an already mentioned object :

τὸ τεῖχος περιεῖλον τὸ καινόν, they destroyed the new wall.

(a) The order, noun, article, adjective, emphasises the adjective :

ἀρετῆς ἕνεκα καὶ προθυμίας τῆς ἐν ἐκείνοις τοῖς κινδύνοις γενομένης.
For the sake of their valour and the zeal which they showed in those dangers.

(b) Adverbs of time and place are used in this position as adjectives :

οἱ νῦν ἄνδρες, the men of to-day.

So also ἄγαν, λίαν, 'excessive', πάνυ, 'celebrated', ἄντικρυς, 'downright', καθάπαξ, 'out and out'.

(c) A defining genitive stands most commonly between the article and the noun, *e.g.* ἡ τοῦ πατρὸς οἰκία, 'the father's house'; it commonly comes after the noun with the repeated article and sometimes (for emphasis) before the article and noun.

So with defining adverb phrases :

ἡ ἐν Μαραθῶνι μάχη or ἡ μάχη ἡ ἐν Μαραθῶνι.
The battle at (of) Marathon.

The article is not repeated with a verbal noun :

ἡ τῶν τυράννων κατάλυσις ἐκ τῆς Ἑλλάδος.
The removal of the tyrants from Greece.

(d) The partitive genitive follows or precedes the article and noun : it is never used with the repeated article :

οἱ δεινότατοι τῶν ῥητόρων, the cleverest of the speakers.

It may be in the attributive position if the last word is a participle or adjective :

αἱ ἄριστα τῶν νεῶν πλέουσαι, the best sailing ships.

(e) The genitives of personal pronouns (except the reflexive) stand *after* the article and noun :

ἡ οἰκία ὑμῶν (αὐτοῦ), your (his) house.
τὸν ἑαυτοῦ πατέρα, his own father.

But :

εἰς τὴν ἐκείνων πόλιν, to the city of those men.

(f) Possessive pronouns (adjectives) stand between the article and the noun : ὁ ἐμὸς πατήρ, 'my father'. But note δοῦλος ὑμέτερος, 'a slave of yours'; and as predicate : σοὶ δοῦλοί ἐσμεν, 'we are your slaves'.

(g) τοιοῦτος, τοιόσδε, τοσοῦτος, τοσόσδε, τηλικοῦτος stand in the attributive position : the article is used when the idea of a definite kind is prominent :

ὁ τοιοῦτος ἀνήρ, such a man as this.

(h) Note also :

ὁ ἄλλος, the rest.
οἱ ἄλλοι, the others. } See also Pronouns.
ὁ ἕτερος, the one or the other of two.
οἱ πολλοί, the majority.
τὸ πολύ, the greater part.
ὁ Εὐφράτης ποταμός, the river Euphrates.

So usually with rivers and mountains, but not cities. The indefinite δεῖνα, 'such a one', always has the article in the attributive position, ὁ δεῖνα, τὸν δεῖνα, etc.

(2) The *Predicative Adjective* precedes the article or follows the noun without taking the article :

σοφὸς ὁ ἀνήρ or ὁ ἀνὴρ σοφός, the man (is) wise.

GREEK PROSE USAGE

(a) This is the position of the demonstrative pronouns οὗτος, ἐκεῖνος, ὅδε.

With another adjective we have:

αὕτη ἡ στενὴ ὁδός.
This narrow road.
(Sometimes ἡ στενὴ αὕτη ὁδός.)
ἐπὶ τὰς ἐξαίφνης ταύτας ἀπὸ τῆς οἰκείας χώρας αὐτοῦ στρατείας.
To meet these sudden expeditions of his from his native land.

The demonstrative (ταύτας) may be put in the attributive position when an attributive word (ἐξαίφνης) follows the article and precedes the demonstrative; another attribute following the demonstrative does not need the article (ἀπὸ τῆς ... χώρας).

(b) A predicative adjective with noun and article is used for an indefinite noun with an adjective:

> τὸ σῶμα θνητὸν ἔχομεν.
> We have a mortal body.
> πόσον ἄγει τὸ στράτευμα;
> How great an army is he bringing?
> ὡς διὰ φιλίας τῆς χώρας.
> As through a friendly country.

(c) The predicative position is used with ἑκάτερος, ἄμφω, ἀμφότεροι, ἕκαστος; but with ἕκαστος the article may be omitted:

> ἐν ἑκάστῃ τῇ πόλει or ἐν ἑκάστῃ πόλει, in each city.

(d) It is also the position for personal pronouns, except the reflexive. See (1) (e).

(e) ἄκρος, 'the top of', μέσος, 'the middle of', ἔσχατος, 'the extremity of', have the predicative position:

> ἐπ' ἄκροις τοῖς ποσίν, on tip-toe.
> διὰ μέσης τῆς πόλεως, through the middle of the city.

(f) Usually πᾶς, σύμπας and ὅλος have the predicative position.

> πάντες οἱ στρατιῶται, all the soldiers.

But:

πᾶσα πόλις, every city.

(i)
πᾶσα ἡ πόλις or ὅλη ἡ πόλις, all the city.

(ii)
ἡ πᾶσα πόλις or ἡ ὅλη πόλις, the whole city.

(i) Contrasts the whole with part; (ii) contrasts the state with the individuals:

οἱ πάντες, in all.
οἱ πάντες στρατιῶται δισχίλιοι, 2000 soldiers in all.

(g) ἥμισυς, ἡμίσεια, ἥμισυ, 'half'.
  (i) as attributive adjective:

ἡ ἡμίσεια πόλις, half the city.

  (ii) With the noun in the genitive:

ἡ ἡμίσεια τῆς πόλεως, half the city.
ὁ ἥμισυς τοῦ στρατοῦ, half the army.

  (iii) In the neuter with the noun in the genitive:

τὸ ἥμισυ τῆς πόλεως, half the city.

NOTE.—The second construction is always used when it means 'half the number':

ἔπεμψε τὰς ἡμισείας τῶν νεῶν, he sent half the ships.

(h) Note the following adverbial adjectives:

σκοταῖος, in the dark.   ἄπρακτος, without success.
ἑσπέριος, in the evening.   ἑβδομαῖος, on the seventh day.
ἄκων, unintentionally.
ἄσμενος, ἑκών, ἡδόμενος, gladly.
πρῶτος αὐτοὺς εἶδον, I was the first to see them.
πρώτους αὐτοὺς εἶδον, they were the first I saw.

See also Participles.

(3) The adjective with the article, singular or plural, denotes a class:

οἱ ἀγαθοί, the good (good men).

In the singular the masculine adjective without the article is rarely used; so ἀνὴρ ἀγαθός = 'a good man'.

(4) A noun may be understood, *e.g.* δεξιά, 'the right hand', τὴν ταχίστην, 'in the quickest way'. See also The Article (5):

> ἡ μουσική (τέχνη), the art of music.
> τὴν πρώτην, at first.

(5) *Neuter adjectives* are used for adverbs, *e.g.* πολλά, 'frequently', μέγα, 'loudly', ἡδύ, 'sweetly'.

(6) The *Descriptive Adjective*:

My aged mother, ἡ ἐμὴ μήτηρ, γραῦς οὖσα.
The gallant commander, ὁ στρατηγὸς ἀνδρεῖος ὤν or ἀνὴρ ἀνδρεῖος.
The friendly king, ὁ βασιλεὺς φίλος ὤν.

NOTE.—This adjective is different from the defining or distinguishing adjective.

(7) With abstract nouns like ἀσφάλεια, προθυμία, ἀθυμία, use πολλή, not μεγάλη, for 'great'.

(8) For agreement of the adjective see Subject and Predicate.

(9) ὡς, ὅτι with superlatives:

> ὡς ἄριστοι, as good as possible.

THE ADVERB

(1) ADVERBIAL adjectives, such as σκοταῖος, 'in the dark'. See p. 74 (h).

(2) Adverbs for attributive adjectives, e.g. οἱ νῦν, 'the men of to-day'. See p. 71 (b).

(3) (i) ὡς with positive adverbs: ὡς ἀληθῶς, 'truly', ὡς ἑτέρως, 'otherwise', ὡσαύτως, 'in like manner', θαυμαστῶς (θαυμασίως, ὑπερφυῶς) ὡς ἀληθῶς, 'in a wonderfully true way'.

(ii) ὡς (ὅτι) with superlative adverbs: ὡς μάλιστα, 'as much as possible', ὡς ἐκ πλείστου, 'at as great a distance (or time) as possible'.

(4) ἔχω with an adverb means 'I am': καλῶς ἔχω 'I am well'. Also ὡς εἶχε τάχους ἕκαστος, 'as quickly as each could'.

(5) The adjective is used for English adverb: ἑκών, 'willingly'. See p. 74 (h).

(6) Note adverbs like ἑκατέρωθεν, 'on both sides', used as prepositions with genitive (see The Uses of the Prepositions).

(7) The enclitic πως, 'somehow or other', is frequently added to adjectives and adverbs: ὡδί πως, 'in some such way as this', οὕτω πως, 'just like this, simply'. Also εἴ πως, 'if haply, to see if' (see Further Notes on Conditional Sentences, p. 29 (iii)).

THE ARTICLE

(1) THE *indefinite article* may be translated by the enclitic τις (indefinite pronoun). See The Pronouns:

δοῦλός τις, a (certain) slave.

(2) The *definite article*, used as in English = 'the'. It is required in Greek, though not in English:

(a) To denote a class:

αἱ γυναῖκες, women.

Also in singular:

ὁ σύμβουλος, $\left.{a \atop the}\right\}$ statesman (= statesmen as a class).

(b) With abstract nouns:

ἡ ἀρετή, virtue.

(c) With proper nouns, *e.g.*, names of countries:

ἡ Ἑλλάς, Greece.

With names of men it is optional.

(d) With possessive and demonstrative adjectives. See The Adjective.

(3) The article is omitted in Greek:

(a) In the predicate even with a superlative or a possessive adjective:

οὗτος ἐμὸς ἑταῖρος ἦν, this man was my comrade.
μία αὕτη ὁδὸς ὀρθία, this is the only straight road.

But if the predicate refers to distinct persons or things, it may have the article:

εἰσὶ δ' οὗτοι οἱ εἰδότες τἀληθές;
Are these they who know the truth?

(b) With βασιλεύς, the 'King of Persia'.

(c) In expressions of time and place, e.g.:

νυκτός, by night.
ἅμα ἕῳ, at daybreak.
ἐν ἀγορᾷ, in the market-place.
περὶ ἡλίου δυσμάς, at sunset.

κατὰ γῆν, by land.
κατὰ θάλασσαν, by sea.
εἰς πόλιν, to town.

(d) With some abstracts, when regarded as general conceptions:

οὐδέποτε λυσιτελέστερον ἀδικία δικαιοσύνης.
Injustice is never more profitable than justice.

(4) The article is sometimes used with numbers:

τὰ δύο μέρη, two-thirds.

Especially with ἀμφί, εἰς, 'about', e.g.:

ἡμέρας ἀμφὶ τὰς τριάκοντα, about thirty days.

It is used in distributive expressions:

τοῦ μηνός, per month, a month.

(5) Nouns like γῆ, υἱός, πράγματα are often omitted:

εἰς τὴν ἑαυτῶν, to their own land.
τὰ τῆς πόλεως, the affairs of the city.
Ἀλέξανδρος ὁ τοῦ Φιλίππου, Alexander, son of Philip.

(6) The article is used with the participle for a relative clause. See The Uses of the Participles.

(7) (a) The *neuter article* with the infinitive is the gerund. See The Uses of the Infinitive.

(b) With the accusative and infinitive it equals *the fact that*. See The Uses of the Infinitive.

(c) It is used with an indirect question:

περὶ τοῦ ὅντινα τρόπον χρὴ ζῆν.
About the question how to live.

(d) It is used in quotation:

τὸ ὑμεῖς, the word ὑμεῖς.
τὸ γνῶθι σαυτόν, the expression 'know thyself'.

GREEK PROSE USAGE

(e) With the genitive it is often a mere periphrasis :

τὸ τῶν πρεσβυτέρων ἡμῶν, as for us elders.

(8) With two or more nouns joined by 'and', the article need not be repeated if they form one idea :

οἱ στρατηγοὶ καὶ λοχαγοί, the generals and captains.

(9) The article is used pronominally :

ὁ μέν . . . ὁ δέ, the one . . . the other.
οἱ μέν . . . οἱ δέ, some . . . others.
τὸ μέν (τὰ μέν) . . . τὸ δέ (τὰ δέ), partly . . . partly.
ὁ δέ, and, but, he (of a fresh subject).
τὸν δὲ εἰπεῖν λέγεται, but it is said that he said.
τὸ καὶ τό, this and that.
τὸν καὶ τόν, this man and that (object).
πρὸ τοῦ, formerly.
τῷ, therefore.

(10) The article at the beginning of a clause may be separated from its noun by μέν, δέ, τε, γάρ, γε, δή, οὖν.

PRONOUNS

(1) PERSONAL PRONOUNS.—(*a*) The nominatives are seldom used, except for emphasis.

(*b*) The forms ἐμέ, ἐμοῦ, ἐμοί are more emphatic than the enclitics με, μου, μοι. The enclitic forms are not used with prepositions, except πρός με.

(*c*) The third person pronoun (ἕ, οὗ, οἷ, etc.) is used as the indirect reflexive, only οἷ in the singular being found in prose, but ἑαυτόν or αὐτόν is generally used for the indirect reflexive:

> ἐννοούμενοι ὅτι προυδεδώκεσαν αὐτοὺς οἱ βάρβαροι.
> Reflecting that the natives had betrayed them.

But:

> The Spartans gave the Aeginetans the district of Thyrea, ὅτι σφῶν εὐεργέται ἦσαν, because they had helped them (the Spartans).
>
> εἶπε τοῖς Ἀθηναίοις ὅτι Ἀρχίδαμος μέν οἱ ξένος εἴη.
> He told the Athenians that Archidamus was his friend.

(2) INTENSIVE PRONOUN, αὐτός.—(*a*) In all cases αὐτός means 'self', used in the predicative position:

> αὐτὸς ὁ στρατηγός, the general himself.

(*b*) In all cases it means 'same', used in the attributive position:

> τὰ αὐτά (ταὐτά).
> The same things.
>
> τὸ Κλέωνος τὸ αὐτὸ δίκαιον καὶ ξύμφορον.
> What is at the same time right and expedient for Cleon.

(*c*) In the oblique cases αὐτόν, etc., means 'him, her, it', etc. It also stands for the indirect reflexive, as in (1) (*c*).

NOTE.—δέκατος αὐτός, 'with nine others' (denoting

the chief in command). αὐτοῖς (τοῖς) ἀνδράσιν, 'with men and all' (dative of accompaniment). αὐτὸς ἔφη, 'the master said it' (*ipse dixit*) (used by slaves of their masters, wives of husband, children of parents, pupils of teachers).

(3) REFLEXIVE PRONOUNS.—These correspond almost exactly to the English 'myself, yourself', etc. They are often strengthened by a preceding αὐτός:

> οἷός τε αὐτὸς ἑαυτῷ βοηθεῖν, able to help himself.

They may be used for the reciprocal pronoun ἀλλήλους, 'one another':

> ἑαυτοῖς διαλέγεσθαι, to converse with one another.

(4) POSSESSIVE PRONOUNS.—(*a*) First and second persons:

> ὁ ἐμὸς πατήρ or ὁ πατήρ μου, my father.

Note the attributive position for the adjective, but the predicative for the genitive: the enclitic form μου is used, not ἐμοῦ. In the plural ἡμῶν, ὑμῶν are less common than ὁ ἡμέτερος, ὁ ὑμέτερος.

Note also:

> πολίτας ὑμετέρους ἄγων, carrying off citizens of yours.
> θυγατέρα σὴν γῆμαι, to marry one of your daughters.
> τὴν ὑμετέραν τῶν σοφιστῶν τέχνην, the art of you sophists.
> τὸν ἡμέτερον αὐτῶν πατέρα, our own father.

But:

> τὸν ἐμαυτοῦ πατέρα, my own father.

And so generally for the singular in prose.

(*b*) The third person, 'his, her, their', is omitted if it refers to the subject and is not emphatic. If emphatic it is translated by ἑαυτοῦ, etc., in the attributive position:

> τοὺς ἑαυτοῦ παῖδας, his own children.

But τὸ εὐώνυμον κέρας ἑαυτῶν, 'their own left wing', because of the epithet. If it does not refer to the subject it is translated by αὐτοῦ, etc., in the predicative position:

> τοὺς παῖδας αὐτοῦ, his children.

σφέτερος is the indirect reflexive:

> The Plataeans attack the invading Thebans at night, ὅπως ἥσσους ὦσι τῆς σφετέρας ἐμπειρίας, in order that the Thebans may be inferior to their (the Plataeans') knowledge of the city.

(5) DEMONSTRATIVE PRONOUNS.—οὗτος, ὅδε, 'this', ἐκεῖνος, 'that', take the article in the predicative position:

> οὗτος ὁ παῖς, this boy.

οὗτος usually in the historians refers to what is past, though elsewhere it often refers to what follows. It may express contempt, when used with a proper noun or ἀνήρ.

It is also exclamatory:

> οὗτος, τί ποιεῖς; You there, what are you doing?

Also deictic (without the article):

> ξένοι οὗτοι, ἐνθάδε, see, here are foreigners.

NOTE.—τοῦτο μέν, 'in the first place . . .', τοῦτο δέ, 'secondly'. τοιοῦτος, 'such', τοσοῦτος, 'so great', οὕτως, 'thus', are used like οὗτος.

ὅδε refers to what follows: so also τοιόσδε, τοσόσδε and ὧδε:

> τοιόνδε ἐμηχανᾶτο, he devised the following trick.

τηλικοῦτος and τηλικόσδε mean 'so old or so large'. ἐκεῖνος, 'that', is also used for an emphatic 'he, she, it'.

NOTES.—(i) The Greek for 'those who' is usually the article with the participle.
But:

> ἃ ἐβούλετο (ταῦτα) ἔλαβε.
> What he wanted, he took.
> ταῦτα ἃ ἐβούλετο ἔλαβε.
> He took these things, which he wanted.

(ii)

ὁ ἕτερος (ἅτερος), neuter θάτερον, the one or the other of two.
οἱ ἕτεροι, the rest.
ἕτερον ποτήριον, a different cup.

(iii) The demonstrative is often attracted to the gender and number of a predicative noun :

αὕτη πενία ἐστὶ σαφής (for τοῦτο), this is plain poverty.

But it remains neuter when emphatic :

τοῦτο πῶς οὐκ ἀμαθία ἐστίν; *this* is surely ignorance.

(iv) The demonstrative with a predicative adjective occurs thus :

ταῦτα ἀληθῆ λέγω, this that I say is true.
τί τοῦτο λέγεις; What do you mean by this ?

(v) οὗτος, ὅδε, in apposition, mean 'here', ἐκεῖνος, 'there'.

οὗτος προσέρχεται, here he comes.
νῆες ἐκεῖναι ἐπιπλέουσιν, ships are sailing up yonder.

See also Deictic use above.

(vi) The demonstratives are emphasized by adding iota (ί), before which a short vowel is dropped, *e.g.* οὑτοσί, τουτί.

(vii) The article may be omitted with demonstratives when a relative clause follows :

ἐπὶ γῆν τήνδε, ἐν ᾗ ἐκράτησαν.
To this land, in which they overcame . . .

(6) THE INTERROGATIVE PRONOUN.—τίς, 'who ?' is used either as a pronoun or adjective :

τίνας (ἄνδρας) εἶδον; Whom (what men) did I see ?

τίς is used for the indirect interrogative, but ὅστις is more common, and so for ποῖος, etc.

(7) THE INDEFINITE PRONOUN.—τις (enclitic), 'some, any', used either as pronoun or adjective.

τοῦτο λέγει τις, someone says this.
κλέπτης τις, a sort of thief.

It is often equivalent to the English indefinite article :

> ἀνήρ τις, a (certain) man.
> τριάκοντά τινες, some thirty.
> σχεδόν τι, very nearly.
> εἶναί τι, to be someone of importance.

NOTES.—(i) τις may be added to οἷος, ὅσος, ὁποῖος, ὁπόσος, ὁπότερος to make them indefinite :

> ὁποῖός τις, of what kind soever.

(ii) οὖν added to a relative gives it an indefinite meaning :

> ὁστισοῦν, ὁτιοῦν, any whatever (=every).

(iii) πᾶς τις, like ἕκαστος, means 'each, every' (of any number).

(iv) δεῖνα, always with the article, means 'so and so' :

> ὁ δεῖνα, τὸν δεῖνα, etc., such a one.

(v) τις means 'people generally' :

> τὸ λυπῆσαί τινα, boring people.

(vi) τις is contemptuous or minatory :

ἔστι τις Σωκράτης, there is one Socrates.
ἐάν τις ἐπ' αὐτοὺς ἴῃ, if anyone (*i.e.* Philip) should attack them.

(vii) It has a collective sense :

> μισεῖ τις ἐκεῖνον, many a man hates him.

(8) THE RELATIVE PRONOUN.—See separate chapter.
(9) OTHER PRONOMINAL ADJECTIVES.—
(a)
> ἄλλος, other.
> οἱ ἄλλοι, the rest.
> ἄλλοι (οἱ μέν) . . . ἄλλοι (οἱ δέ), some . . . others.
> ἄλλοι ἄλλα δρῶσι, they do different things.
> ἡ ἄλλη πόλις, the rest of the city.
> ἄλλο ποτήριον, another (one more) cup.
> οὐδὲν ἄλλο ἤ, simply, absolutely.

οὐδὲν ἄλλο ἢ ἀναμιμνήσκονται { they do nothing else than remember.
{ they simply remember.

(b) ἕκαστος, 'each', with predicative article or without article :

> τὸ αὐτῆς ἑκάστῃ ἔργον, each her own work.
> ὡς ἕκαστοι, severally.
> ἐν ἑκάστῃ τῇ πόλει or ἐν ἑκάστῃ πόλει, in each city.

καθ' ἕκαστον (or καθ' ἕνα) is used instead of a case of ἕκαστος :

> τὸ καθ' ἕκαστον περικόπτειν τῶν Ἑλλήνων.
> Fleecing the Greeks one after another.

(c) ἑκάτερος (with the predicative article), 'each of two' :

> ἐφ' ἑκατέρῳ τῷ κέρᾳ, on both wings.

(d) ἄμφω, ἀμφότεροι (with the predicative article), 'both'.

The plural is often used instead of the dual :

> ἀμφότεροι οἱ στρατηγοί, both generals.

Similarly the plural of the verb is used with a dual subject.

(10) THE RECIPROCAL PRONOUN.—ἀλλήλους, 'one another, each other', used only in oblique cases of dual and plural.

The reflexive pronouns (ἡμᾶς αὐτούς, ἑαυτούς, etc.) can be used as the reciprocal :

> ἑαυτῶν πυνθάνεσθαι.
> To learn of one another.
> κακῶς ἔχοντες πρὸς ἑαυτούς.
> Being on bad terms with one another.

(11) NEGATIVE PRONOMINAL ADJECTIVES :

> οὐδείς, μηδείς, no one, none, no.
> οὐδὲ εἷς, no single one, not a man.
> οὐδέτερος, μηδέτερος, neither.

(12) NEGATIVE ADVERBS :

> οὐδέποτε, μηδέποτε, never.
> οὐδαμοῦ, μηδαμοῦ, nowhere.
> οὐδαμῶς, μηδαμῶς, in no way, manner.

(13) Table of Pronouns and Adverbs

(1) Interrogative	(2) Indirect Interrogative	(3) Demonstrative	(4) Relative	(5) Indefinite
τίς; who?	ὅστις	οὗτος, ὅδε, ἐκεῖνος	ὅς	τις
πόσος; how much?	ὁπόσος	τοσοῦτος, τοσόσδε	ὅσος	ποσός
ποῖος; of what sort?	ὁποῖος	τοιοῦτος, τοιόσδε	οἷος	ποιός
πότερος; which of two?	ὁπότερος	ἕτερος	ὁπότερος	—
πηλίκος; {how old? how large?}	ὁπηλίκος	πηλικοῦτος, πηλικόσδε	ἡλίκος	—
ποῦ; where?	ὅπου	ἐνθάδε, ἐκεῖ	οὗ	που
ποῖ; whither?	ὅποι	δεῦρο, ἐκεῖσε	οἷ	ποι
πόθεν; whence?	ὁπόθεν	ἐνθένδε, ἐκεῖθεν	ὅθεν	ποθέν
πότε; when?	ὁπότε	τότε	ὅτε	ποτέ
πῶς; how?	ὅπως	ὧδε, οὕτως	ὡς	πως
πῇ; in which way?	ὅπῃ	τῇδε, ταύτῃ	ᾗ	πῃ

In direct questions use the forms in column (1).
In indirect questions use the forms in column (2), less commonly (1), sometimes (4).
In relative clauses use the forms in column (4) or (2).
In exclamations use the forms in column (4).

SUBJECT AND PREDICATE

(1) THE subject of a finite verb is in the nominative case: the verb agrees with its subject in number and person, but with a plural neuter subject, the verb is in the singular, except when the noun denotes persons, e.g. τὰ τέλη, 'the authorities'.

NOTES.—(i) A dual subject often has a verb in the plural, when no stress is laid on precisely *two*.

(ii) A singular collective noun (e.g. πλῆθος) may take a plural verb, with agreement in the natural gender:

> πολὺ γένος ἀνθρώπων τρεφόμενοι ζῶσιν.
> A large part of mankind are nurtured and live.

(iii) With two or more subjects of different persons the verb is in the 1st or 2nd person plural, except when it conforms to the nearest subject for emphasis:

> σύ τε Ἕλλην εἶ καὶ ἡμεῖς.
> σύ τε καὶ ἡμεῖς Ἕλληνές ἐσμεν.
> You and we are Greeks.

With several subjects of the 3rd person the verb may be singular, conforming to the nearest object:

> οἱ πένητες καὶ ὁ δῆμος πλέον ἔχει.
> The poor and the common people have the advantage.

If the subjects are things, of the same gender or of different genders, the verb is often singular, as for a plural neuter subject, with a neuter predicative adjective:

> πόλεμος καὶ στάσις ὀλέθριά ἐστιν.
> War and civil strife are baneful (things).

(iv) With subjects separated by ἤ, 'or', and οὔτε ... οὔτε, 'neither ... nor', the verb conforms to the nearest.

(v) Copulative verbs (*e.g.* εἰμί, γίγνομαι, καλοῦμαι) conform to their predicate when it is a noun :

> τὸ χωρίον ἐννέα ὁδοὶ ἐκαλοῦντο.
> The place was called Nine Ways.

(vi) The words ἄλλος, ἕκαστος and the like are used in apposition to a plural subject without affecting the verb, but the verb may conform to the appositive word when that word precedes the verb :

> οὗτοι ἄλλος ἄλλα λέγουσιν or λέγει.
> These men say different things.

(vii) A 3rd person plural subject is sometimes omitted when it refers to men in general :

> καλοῦσιν, men call.

(viii) The 2nd person is used for an indefinite subject in hypothetical sentences with ἄν (potential) :

> οὐκ ἂν εὗρες, you (one) would not have found,

and after ἐάν or a relative with ἄν and the subjunctive :

> ὅσῳ ἂν μᾶλλον παρακελεύῃ, the more you urge (one urges).

(ix) The subject of the infinitive mood is in the accusative, but it is omitted when it is the same as the subject of the main verb, and predicative words agree in the nominative case :

> οἴονται δεινοὶ εἶναι, they think they are clever.

A demonstrative pronoun when subject usually agrees in gender with a predicate noun, but we find :

> τοῦτο δ' ἔστ' οὐχ ἣν οὑτωσί τις ἂν φήσειεν ἀτιμίαν.
> This is not the outlawry commonly meant.

See also Pronouns 5 (iii), p. 83.

(2) *The Predicate or Complement*

A. The verbs 'to be, to become, to be made' and the

GREEK PROSE USAGE

like have a complement, noun or adjective, in the same case as the subject.

NOTES.—(i) The predicative adjective is neuter with a masculine or feminine subject when it 'denotes the essence of a certain class':

> ἀσθενέστερον γυνὴ ἀνδρός.
> Woman is a weaker thing than man.

(ii) With several singular subjects, being persons, the predicative adjective is masculine plural, if the persons are of different gender; but it often conforms to the nearest subject, as does the verb:

> καὶ ὁ ἀνὴρ καὶ ἡ γυνὴ ἀγαθοί εἰσιν.
> Both the husband and wife are good.

(iii) With several singular subjects, being things, the predicative adjective agrees with the nearest or is made dual or plural:

> ἡ στάσις καὶ ὁ πόλεμος αἴτιός ἐστιν.
> Strife and war are the cause.

If the subjects are of different genders (or even of the same gender) the adjective is neuter plural with a singular verb, as in (1) Note (iii).

(iv) For the predicative adjective used for adverb see The Adjective (2) (*h*).

(v) A neuter adjective in the plural (for singular) is found with the verb 'to be':

> ἀδύνατα ἦν, it was impossible.

(vi) Local adverbs are found as complements of the verb 'to be', *e.g.*:

> μακράν, χωρὶς εἶναι, to be far off, apart.

Also μάτην, 'in vain', ἅλις, 'enough'. The verb 'to be' is used impersonally with adverbs, *e.g.*:

> καλῶς ἔσται, it will be well.

B. The complement of an infinitive usually agrees with its antecedent in the main clause; otherwise it is in the accusative, since the subject of the infinitive is in the accusative, except when it is the same as the subject of the main verb:

> ἀντὶ τοῦ ἐπελθεῖν αὐτοί, βούλεσθε ...
> Instead of yourselves attacking, you prefer ...
>
> ἔξεστιν ἡμῖν ἀπιέναι τὰ ὅπλα ἔχουσιν (ἔχοντας).
> We may go away with the arms.

But with the participle, the complement always agrees with the antecedent:

> τῶν φασκόντων σοφῶν εἶναι.
> Of those who assert that they are wise.

NOTE.—An exception is εἶναί τι, 'to be someone of importance', which is never changed.

APPOSITION

A NOUN which describes another noun or pronoun is in apposition to it and is put in the same case :

>ὑμεῖς, οἱ σοφοί, you, the wise ones.
>Θεμιστοκλῆς ἥκω, I, Themistocles, am come.

NOTES.—(i) Apposition is possible to nouns in the nominative or accusative (and sometimes in other cases), e.g. :

>σὺν σοὶ φίλῳ, with you as friend.

(ii) A word indicating a relation of time has ὤν :

>παῖς ὤν, as a child.

(iii) Apposition is not used with objects not in the accusative, except with χρῶμαι and τυγχάνω :

>τυχεῖν τινος φίλου, to gain someone as a friend.
>χρῆσθαί τινι φίλῳ, to treat someone as a friend.

(iv) Otherwise ὡς, ὥσπερ, καθάπερ must be used, with the nominative (as subject of verb understood) or with the case of the preceding noun or pronoun.

(v) With λέγω, 'I mean', the appositive word is put in the same case as the preceding word or in the accusative, as object of λέγω.

(vi) A noun, instead of being in the partitive genitive, may be in the same case as the words that signify the parts :

>οἰκίαι αἱ μὲν πολλαί . . . ὀλίγαι δέ . . .
>Of the houses, most . . . but a few . . .

(vii) ἀνήρ is often used with words denoting station or condition, e.g. ἀνὴρ ἄρχων, ἀνὴρ τύραννος, 'a ruler, a tyrant'.

(viii) Limiting apposition :

Πελοποννήσιοι καὶ οἱ σύμμαχοι τὰ δύο μέρη.
The Peloponnesians and their allies (two-thirds of them).

(ix) A noun may stand in apposition to a sentence, usually in the accusative case :

ἐπιγεγένηται ἡ νόσος ἥδε, πρᾶγμα ἐλπίδος κρεῖσσον.
This plague has come upon us, an unexpected affair.

THE USES OF THE CASES

THE *Nominative* is the subject of a finite verb, the complement of the verb 'to be' (and the like) and the subject and complement of the infinitive, when the same as the subject of the main verb. See Subject and Predicate.

The *Vocative*, used in addressing a person or thing, takes ὦ in prose, except for 'forcible brevity'. An adjective is put between ὦ and the noun when emphatic, *e.g.* ὦ καλὲ παῖ, otherwise after it, *e.g.* ὦ Πρώταρχε φίλε. It is always after the noun in customary forms of address, *e.g.* ὦ ἄνδρες Ἀθηναῖοι.

NOTE.—The Nominative is sometimes used as Vocative.

The *Accusative* is the case of the direct object of a transitive verb. Verbs transitive in English may govern the genitive or dative in Greek: verbs intransitive in English may be transitive in Greek, *e.g.* ὄμνυμι + accusative, 'I swear by'. Both classes of verbs must be learnt by practice. Greek intransitive verbs usually become transitive when compounded with the prepositions διά, μετά, παρά, περί, ὑπέρ, ὑπό, κατά: *e.g.* βαίνω, διαβαίνω, εἶμι (*ibo*), διέξειμι, πάρειμι.

The accusative for genitive is found after nouns and adjectives formed from verbs:

τὰ μετέωρα φροντιστής, an observer of heavenly things.

Verbs of asking (ἐρωτάω), demanding (αἰτέω, πράττω), teaching (διδάσκω), concealing (κρύπτω), reminding (ἀναμιμνήσκω), clothing and unclothing (ἀμφιέννυμι, ἐκδύω), depriving (ἀποστερέω), taking away (ἀφαιροῦμαι), may take *two accusatives*.

τοὺς δὲ ἄλλους ἀφελόμενοι τὴν ναῦν.
Taking the ship away from the others.

NOTES.—(i) ἐρωτάω usually takes περί τινος (about something):

ἀναμιμνῄσκω }
ἀποστερέω } may take a genitive of the thing.

ἀφαιροῦμαι may take a genitive of the person.

(ii) So also:

> κακὰ λέγειν + accusative, to speak ill of.
> κακὰ ποιεῖν + accusative, to do ill to.
> Otherwise εὖ (κακῶς) λέγειν, ποιεῖν + accusative.

πράττω is not used for ποιῶ in this way. εὖ πράττειν means 'to be well off'. The passive of εὖ ποιεῖν is εὖ πάσχειν. The passive of εὖ λέγειν is εὖ ἀκούειν.

(iii) One of the two accusatives may be retained in the passive:

> οὐδὲν ἄλλο διδάσκεται ἄνθρωπος, a man is taught nothing else.

(iv) Verbs of making, thinking, naming, choosing, appointing, take a direct object and an object-complement:

> στρατηγὸν αὐτὸν ἀπέδειξαν, they appointed him general.

In the passive they take a complement in the nominative:

> οὗτος στρατηγὸς κατέστη, this man was appointed general.

Other Uses of the Accusative

(1) The *Cognate Accusative* (of kindred meaning), used with transitive or intransitive verbs:

> νικᾶν Ἴσθμια, to win at the Isthmian games.
> γραφὴν διώκειν (+ accusative), to prosecute.

Also with adjectives, *e.g.* κακοὶ πᾶσαν κακίαν, 'bad with all badness', and in the passive, *e.g.* τὰ πεπολιτευμένα, 'public acts', τὰ ἡμαρτημένα, 'errors'.

(2) The *Internal Accusative*:

> τὰ δίκαια βοηθῆσαι, to render just aid.

χρῆσθαί τινί τι.
To use something (dative) for something (accusative).
(Usually *χρῆσθαί τινι ἐπί* + accusative.)
πολλὰ ὑμᾶς ἠδίκησε.
He did you many wrongs.

(3) Many expressions in the accusative are used with adverbial force, *e.g.* :

αὐτὰ ταῦτα, for this very reason.
τοῦτον τὸν τρόπον, in this way (also *τούτῳ τῷ τρόπῳ*).
πάντα τρόπον, πᾶσαν ἰδέαν, in every way.
τέλος, finally.
τὰ ἄλλα, in other respects.
ἐμὴν χάριν, for my sake.
τὸ κατ' ἐμέ, for my part.

(4) *Extent of Time and Space.*—(*a*) Time how long :

ἡμέρας πέντε, for five days.

Time how long ago, with the ordinal, by inclusive reckoning :

ἑβδόμην ἡμέραν, six days since.
τρίτον ἔτος τουτί, two years ago.

(*b*) Distance how far :

σταδίους πολλοὺς ἀπέχειν, to be many stades distant.

NOTE.—Eight stades equal one mile.

(5) *Respect or Specification.*—(*a*) With a verb :

κάμνω (ἀλγῶ) τὴν κεφαλήν, I have a headache.

(*b*) With a noun :

Ἕλληνες τὸ γένος, Greeks by race.

(*c*) With an adjective :

ἀγαθὸς τέχνην, good at a craft.

(6) The accusative is used after the words *νή, μά* in oaths :

νὴ τὸν Δία, Yes, by Zeus.
(οὐ) μὰ τὸν Δία, No, by Zeus.

but :

ναί, μὰ τὸν Δία, Yes, by Zeus.

THE GENITIVE CASE

(1) *Attributive*, after a noun, generally means 'of'.

(a) Possessive : ἡ τοῦ πατρὸς οἰκία, 'the father's house'.

(b) Subjective : ἡ τοῦ δήμου εὔνοια, 'the goodwill of the people'.

(c) Objective : τὸ Παυσανίου μῖσος, 'hatred of (against) Pausanias'.

(d) Material or Definition : κρήνη ἡδέος ὕδατος, 'a well of fresh water'.

(e) Measure or Age : ὁδὸς τριῶν ἡμερῶν, 'a three days' journey'; ἀνὴρ ἐτῶν τριάκοντα, 'a man of thirty'; ἵππου δρόμος ἡμέρας, 'a day's running of a horse'.

(f) Cause or Origin : γραφὴ ἀσεβείας, 'an indictment for impiety'.

(g) Partitive : πολλοὶ τῶν πολιτῶν, 'many of the citizens'.

NOTES.—(i) With numbers and words like μόνος, ὀλίγοι, the prepositions ἀπό, ἐκ with the genitive are sometimes used.

(ii) ὁ ἥμισυς, 'half', ὁ λοιπός, 'the rest', ὁ πλεῖστος, 'the most', τοῦ χρόνου, 'of the time'. The adjectives take the gender and number of χρόνος.

(iii) After an adverb of place or time or amount :

ποῦ τῆς γῆς;
Where on the earth ?

εἰς τοῦτο ὕβρεως.
To this point of insolence.

οἷ προεληλυθ' ἀσελγείας.
To what a pitch of arrogance he has come.

οὕτω πόρρω προεληλύθασι φυλακῆς.
So far have they gone in caution.

δὶς τῆς ἡμέρας.
Twice a day.

ἐπὶ Φάρσαλον τῆς Θεσσαλίας.
To Pharsalus, in Thessaly.

(iv) With ἔχω (and other verbs) and adverbs like πῶς, ὡς, εὖ, καλῶς, κακῶς, ἱκανῶς :

> ὡς εἶχε τάχους, as fast as he could.
> πῶς ἔχεις δόξης; How are you in opinion ?

The noun in the genitive is always without the article. The name 'Genitive of the sphere in which' is used.

(v) The genitive means 'one of' (also with εἷς) :

> τῶν τριάκοντα ἦν, he was one of the Thirty.

(vi) The genitive expresses an indefinite portion :

> πίνει τοῦ οἴνου, he drinks some wine.
> τῆς γῆς ἔτεμον, they ravaged some of the land.

(vii) Verbs of sharing take a partitive genitive, *e.g.* :

> μετέχω, μέτεστί μοι, I have a share in.
> μεταδίδωμι, I give a share in (+ dative of recipient).
> μεταποιοῦμαι, I claim a share in.

Also :

> ἔλαβον τὸν Ὀρόνταν τῆς ζώνης.
> They seized Orontes by the girdle.

(viii) With the partitive genitive of 1st or 2nd person, the verb is generally 3rd, *e.g.* :

> ἡμῶν οἱ πρεσβύτεροί εἰσιν οὐκ ἄπειροι.
> The elders of us are not without experience.

(2) *Genitive with Verbs.*—(*a*) Verbs of seizing, touching, hitting, missing, beginning and the like.

> καί μου λαβόμενος τοῦ ἱματίου, seizing me by the cloak.

NOTE.—ἄρχομαι ἐκ, ἀπό + genitive = 'I begin with'.

(*b*) Verbs of tasting, smelling, hearing, perceiving, remembering, forgetting, desiring, caring for, sparing, neglecting, wondering at, despising (see also Genitive of Cause) :

> τοσοῦτον τοῦ κινδύνου κατεφρόνησε.
> He despised danger so much.

NOTES.—(i) Verbs of hearing, perceiving and the like may take an accusative of the thing heard and a genitive of the person heard, or heard from. ἀκούω παρά (πρός, ἐκ) is also used for 'I hear from'.

(ii) ἐπίσταμαι, 'I understand', takes the accusative. συνίημι, 'I understand', usually takes the accusative of the thing.

(iii)
> μέλει μοι, I care for + genitive.
> μεταμέλει μοι, I repent of + genitive.
> προσήκει μοι, I have a concern in + genitive.

(iv) μέμνημαι, 'I remember', takes accusative or genitive. ἀναμιμνήσκω, 'I remind', takes accusative and genitive or two accusatives.

(c) Verbs of ruling and leading and the like, e.g. ἄρχω, κρατέω.

NOTE.—ἡγοῦμαι + genitive = 'I rule'; ἡγοῦμαι + dative = 'I show the way'.

(d) Verbs of being full and lacking.

NOTES.—(i) δεῖ (= 'there is need') takes the dative of the person and the genitive of the thing:

> δεῖ μοι = I need = δέομαι.

So:
> πολλοῦ δεῖ, far from it.

and:
> πολλοῦ δέω ἀπολογεῖσθαι, I am far from defending myself.

Do not confuse this use with δεῖ + accusative and infinitive = 'I must'.

(ii) δέομαι (= 'I ask') takes the genitive of the person.

(iii) Verbs of filling take the accusative and genitive.

(e) Verbs of separation, e.g. ἀπέχω, παύομαι, ἀφαιροῦμαι.

NOTE.—Verbs of depriving may take two accusatives. See Uses of the Accusative Case.

> ἀπέχειν (ἀπό) τῆς πόλεως, to be distant from the city.

GREEK PROSE USAGE

(*f*) Verbs of comparison, *e.g.* διαφέρω, περιγίγνομαι, ὑστερίζω :

> ὑστερίζειν τῶν καίρων, to be too late for the opportunity.
> γυναικῶν οὐδὲν διαφέρουσι, they are no better than women.

NOTES.—

(i)

προέχω (ὑπερέχω) τινός τινι, I surpass someone in something.

(ii) ὑπερβάλλω, 'exceed, pass over, cross', takes accusative.

(*g*) Verbs of accusing, acquitting, convicting, condemning, prosecuting, take the accusative of the person and the genitive of the crime or charge.

Such verbs are: αἰτιάομαι, 'accuse', γράφομαι, 'indict', διώκω, 'prosecute', φεύγω, 'am prosecuted', ἁλίσκομαι, 'am convicted', ὀφλισκάνω, 'lose a suit':

> παρανόμων γράφεσθαί τινα.
> To indict someone for illegal proposition.
> φεύγω (ὀφλισκάνω) κλοπῆς.
> I am prosecuted (condemned) for theft.

A cognate accusative, γραφήν, δίκην, is also used :

> οὐδεμίαν ἐγράψατό με γραφήν.
> He commenced no suit against me.
> θανάτου δίκην ὀφλισκάνω.
> I am condemned to death.

NOTE.—ἐγκαλέω, 'accuse', takes the dative of the person and accusative of the charge :

> καὶ τοῦτ' ἔστιν ὃ μοι ἐγκαλεῖς.
> And this is what you accuse me of.

(*h*) If the above verbs are compounds of κατά, they take the accusative of the charge and the genitive of the person. Such verbs are : κατηγορέω, 'accuse', καταγιγνώσκω, 'charge', κατακρίνω, 'condemn', καταψηφίζομαι, 'vote against' :

> κατηγορεῖν ἀδικίαν τινός, to accuse someone of injustice.

GREEK PROSE USAGE

> τί μᾶλλον ἐμοῦ σὺ ταῦτα κατηγορεῖς ἢ ἐγὼ σοῦ;
> Why do you accuse me of this rather than I you?
>
> ἀδικία πολλὴ κατηγορεῖται αὐτοῦ.
> Great injustice is charged against him.
>
> τά μου κατηγορημένα.
> The accusations made against me.

NOTE.—Sometimes these verbs are used personally in the passive:

> καταγνωσθεὶς δειλίαν, being convicted of cowardice.

(*i*) With verbs of emotion, a genitive of cause is used. Such verbs are: θαυμάζω, εὐδαιμονίζω, ζηλόω, στυγέω, φθονέω, οἰκτίρω, ὀργίζομαι:

> τούτους τῆς τόλμης θαυμάζω.
> I wonder at these men for their boldness.

NOTE.—Verbs like θαυμάζω also take a genitive of the person wondered at, as in (2) (*b*):

> τῶν κατηγόρων θαυμάζω, I wonder at my accusers.

Also an accusative of the thing wondered at:

> μηδεὶς τὴν ὑπερβολήν μου θαυμάσῃ.
> Let no one wonder at my exaggeration.

(*j*) Many verbs compounded with πρό, ὑπέρ, ἀπό, ἐκ, ἐπί take the genitive; the preposition may be repeated.

(3) The *Genitive of Exclamation*:

> τῆς τύχης, what a misfortune!

(4) The *Genitive of Price or Value*:

> πόσου διδάσκει; For how much does he teach?

NOTES.—

(i)

τιμᾶν τινί τινος.
To fix a penalty (genitive) for someone (said of the jury).

τιμᾶσθαί τινος.
To propose a penalty (said of the parties to the suit).

(ii)

περὶ πολλοῦ (ὀλίγου, οὐδενός) ποιεῖσθαι, to value highly, etc.

GREEK PROSE USAGE

(iii) The genitive is used for what is paid for :

> τῆς συνουσίας ἀργύριον ἐπράττετο.
> He exacted money for his teaching.

(5) *Genitive of Time.*—Time within which is put in the genitive :

> νυκτός, by night.
> οὐκέτι τοῦ λοιποῦ, no longer in the future.

Also of Place :

> ἰέναι τοῦ πρόσω, to go forward.

(6) The *Elliptic Genitive* with ἐν or εἰς :

> εἰς διδασκάλου, to the schoolmaster's.

Or with εἰμί (*sum*) :

> ἔστιν ἄρα δικαίου ἀνδρὸς βλάπτειν καὶ ὁντινοῦν;
> Is it the part of a just man to injure anyone ?
> τῆς πόλεως εἶναι.
> To belong to the city.

Also :

> ὑμῶν αὐτῶν γενέσθαι, to be your own masters.

(7) The *Genitive of Description*—compare (1) (*e*).—A noun with an adjective in the genitive with the verb 'to be' :

> ταῦτα δαπάνης μεγάλης ἐστί, this is a matter of great expense.

(8) The genitive follows adjectives with meanings similar to those of verbs taking the genitive, *e.g.* :

μέτοχος, sharing in.	μεστός, full of.
ἔμπειρος, experienced in.	κενός, empty of.
ὑπήκοος, obedient to.	διάφορος, distinct from.

NOTES.—(i) Adjectives like ἄπαις, ἄτιμος take the genitive.

(ii) ἄξιος + genitive = 'worthy of' ; ἄξιος + dative = 'worth while to'.

(iii) ἴδιος and adjectives denoting possession take the genitive. κοινός takes genitive or dative.

(iv) ὑπεύθυνος, 'responsible for', ὑποτελής, 'subject to (liable to pay)', take the genitive.

(v) For adverbs of place with the genitive see The Uses of the Prepositions.

(9) *Genitive of Comparison.* See Comparative Clauses.
(10) *Genitive Absolute.* See Participles.
(11) *Genitive of Purpose.* See Infinitive with Article.

THE DATIVE CASE

(1) (*a*) The indirect object, with a transitive verb governing a direct object, is the same as the English 'to' or 'for'; it is found with verbs of giving, promising, telling, showing and the like.

(*b*) Many verbs compounded with ἀντί, ἐν, ἐπί, περί, πρός, σύν, ὑπό take the dative, or the accusative and dative, *e.g.*:

> περιτιθέναι τινὶ στέφανον, to put a crown on someone.

Sometimes the preposition is repeated, *e.g.*:

> ἐμμένω τοῖς ὅρκοις, I abide by the oaths.
> ἐμμένω ἐν τῇ τάξει, I stand fast in the ranks.

The personal indirect object may become the subject in the passive, with a retained accusative, *e.g.*:

> οἱ ἐπιτετραμμένοι τὴν φυλακήν.
> Those entrusted with the guard.

(2) Many verbs govern the dative only.

NOTES.—(i) μέμφομαι + dative = 'I blame':

μέμφομαί τινί τι = I blame something on somebody.

So also ὀνειδίζω, ἐπιτιμάω.

(ii) διαλέγομαι, 'I converse', and μάχομαι, 'I fight', take the dative or πρός + accusative.

(iii) ἕπομαι, 'I follow', takes the dative or μετά + genitive.

GREEK PROSE USAGE

(iv) πιστεύω with accusative and dative means 'I entrust something to someone, I trust someone with something'.

(v) Dative verbs are sometimes used personally in the passive, *e.g.* :

> πολεμοῦνται, they are warred on.
> ἐπιβουλευόμεθα, we are plotted against.
> πιστεύομαι, I am trusted.

(vi) Impersonals like δεῖ, μέτεστι, μέλει, μεταμέλει, προσήκει take a dative of the person and a genitive of the thing. See also Genitive Case.

ἔξεστι, 'it is possible', takes the dative.

(vii) τιμωρέω τινί = 'I avenge someone'; τιμωροῦμαί τινα = 'I punish someone'.

(viii)

> ἐς χεῖρας, ἐς λόγους ἰέναι + dative, to fight, confer with.
> διὰ φιλίας ἰέναι + dative, to be friendly to.

(ix) Different verbs of the same meaning may govern accusative and dative, *e.g.* :

> βοηθέω, I help + dative.
> ὠφελέω, I help + accusative.

(x)

> τί χρήσεται αὐτῷ; What will he use him for ?

(3) The dative is used with adjectives and adverbs having similar meaning to verbs with the dative, *e.g.* :

> ἀκολούθως, in accordance with.
> ἐμποδών (adverb), in the way of.

NOTES.—(i) ἐναντίος, 'opposite', takes dative or genitive.

(ii) Such adjectives, used as nouns, may take the genitive, *e.g.* :

> οἱ ἐκείνου ἔχθιστοι, his bitterest enemies.

(iii) With ὅμοιος, 'similar to', ἴσος, 'equal to', two subjects are coupled by καί (or by the relative):

ὁμοίαν γνώμην ἔχω καὶ σύ, I have a similar opinion to you.

But the second subject is often in the dative:

ὁμοίαν γνώμην ἔχω σοι.
So also : τὰ αὐτὰ φρονῶ σοι (= ἃ σύ).

(iv) Adverbs of place and time, like ἅμα, 'together with', ὁμοῦ, 'with', ἐφεξῆς, 'next', take the dative, e.g.:

ἅμα τῇ ἡμέρᾳ, at daybreak.

(4) The *Dative of Reference or Relation*, denoting a person to whose case a statement is limited:

τί ἐμοὶ καὶ σοί;
What have I to do with you?

ἡ διαβάντι τὸν ποταμὸν πρὸς ἑσπέραν ὁδός.
The road to the west, when you have crossed the river.

ὡς συνελόντι εἰπεῖν.
To speak briefly.

βουλομένῳ (ἡδομένῳ) ἐστὶ τῷ πλήθει.
The multitude is inclined.

ἡμέρα ἦν πέμπτη ἐπιπλέουσιν Ἀθηναίοις.
The Athenians had been five days sailing up.

(5) The *Dative of the Possessor*, with εἰμί and the like:

εἰσὶν ἐμοὶ ξένοι, I have friends.

(6) The *Dative of Cause* (the 'efficient cause'):

ἀγνοίᾳ, through ignorance.
νόσῳ, of disease.

The 'Moving Cause' (= 'on account of') is expressed by διά + accusative.

NOTE.—

γελᾶν ὑφ' ἡδονῆς, to laugh for joy.

(7) The *Dative of Manner*, e.g. παντὶ τρόπῳ, 'in every way'. It is confined to some particular nouns and

adverbial expressions, such as: σιγῇ, 'in silence', λόγῳ, 'in word', ἔργῳ, 'in deed', ἰδίᾳ, 'in private', δημοσίᾳ, 'in public', κοινῇ, 'in common', βίᾳ, 'by force'.

With other words, use the adverb or μετά + genitive or σύν + dative.

Similarly the *Dative of Respect*, e.g. τῷ ὄντι, 'in reality', φύσει, 'by nature' (τὴν φύσιν, 'in natural gifts').

(8) The *Dative of Instrument or Means* (by or with a thing), e.g.:

> τοῖς ὀφθαλμοῖς, with our eyes.

διά + genitive denotes 'by means of'.

NOTE.—
> ζῆν ἀπὸ λείας, to live by plunder.

(9) The *Dative of Accompaniment*, used chiefly of military and naval forces, e.g.:

> εἴκοσι ναυσίν, with twenty ships.
> παμπληθεῖ στόλῳ, with a complete army.
> αὐτοῖς (τοῖς) ἀνδράσιν, with men and all.
> ἀτελεῖ τῇ νίκῃ, with victory incomplete.

(Accompanying circumstances.)

(10) The *Dative of Measure of Difference*, with comparatives:

> πολλῷ, τοσούτῳ, τῷ παντὶ κρεῖττον.
> Much, so much, infinitely better.

NOTES.—(i) πολύ and ὀλίγον are also used and *always* τι, 'somewhat', οὐδέν, 'in no way', e.g. οὐδὲν ἧττον, 'none the less'.

(ii) It is also used with superlatives, e.g. μακρῷ, 'by far', and with πρό, 'before', μετά, 'after':

> δέκα ἔτεσι πρὸ τῆς μάχης, ten years before the battle.

(11) The *Ethic Dative*, used of personal pronouns, with the force of: 'for my sake, I beg you' and the like:

> τούτῳ πάνυ μοι προσέχετε τὸν νοῦν.
> Give your close attention to this, please.

(12) The *Dative of Time When*, usually with 'day, night, month, year' or a festival, *e.g.* :

τῇ ὑστεραίᾳ, on the next day.

With other words ἐν with the dative is generally used, *e.g.* :

ἐν τῷ παρόντι, at present.
ἐν τούτῳ τῷ χρόνῳ, at this time.
So also : ἐν νυκτί, at night.

NOTE.—The article is often omitted with numerals, *e.g.* :

ἐνάτῳ μηνί, in the ninth month.

(13) The *Dative of Agent*, used with the perfect and pluperfect passive and the perfect participle passive when the subject is not personal :

τί πέπρακται τοῖς ἄλλοις; What has been done by the others ?
τὰ πεπραγμένα ἐμαυτῷ, my own exploits.

NOTES.—(i) If the subject of the verb in the passive is personal, the agent is expressed by ὑπό with the genitive.

(ii) This dative is used by Thucydides with other parts of the passive (but rarely) :

τοῖς Κερκυραίοις οὐχ ἑωρῶντο.
They were not seen by the Corcyreans.

THE USES OF THE PREPOSITIONS (IN PROSE)

(1) Prepositions with one case

(a) *Accusative.*—ἀνά, 'up, over, by' (distributive):

> ἀνὰ τὸν ποταμόν, up the river.
> ἀνὰ τέσσαρας, by fours (four deep).

εἰς (ἐς in Thucydides), 'into, to, for':

> ἐσβολαὶ ἐς τὴν Ἀττικήν.
> Invasions into Attica.
> εἰς ἀεί.
> For ever.
> εἰς ἔπειτα.
> Until then.
> πρόνοια ἐς τὸν πόλεμον.
> Forethought for the war.
> ἐς φόβον, ἐς φυγὴν καθίστασθαι.
> To be reduced to fear, to flight, etc.
> ἐς χεῖρας ἐλθεῖν.
> To come to blows.

Expressing the 'end or purpose':

> τάσσεσθαι ὡς ἐς μάχην, to be drawn up for battle.

(b) *Genitive.*—ἀντί, 'instead of, for'; ἀνθ' ὧν, 'wherefore':

> εἰρήνην ἀντὶ πολέμου αἱρεῖσθαι, to choose peace for war.

NOTE.—It is said that ἀντί implies the possession of the thing governed by it: to express a choice between two alternative offers, use πρό with genitive.

ἀπό, 'from' (of place or time):

> εὐθὺς ἀφ' ἑσπέρας, immediately after dusk.
> ἀπὸ τοῦ ἴσου, on equal terms.
> ζῆν ἀπὸ λείας, to live by plunder.

ἐκ, ἐξ, 'from, out of':

> ἐκ τῶν παρόντων.
> With a view to the present state of affairs.
> ἐξ ὀλίγου.
> Suddenly.
> ἐξ ἴσου.
> Equally.
> ἐκ τούτων.
> In consequence of this.
> ἐλεύθερος ἐκ δούλου.
> Free instead of slave.

πρό, 'before (of place or time), on behalf of, instead of':

> πρὸ βασιλέως, on behalf of the king.
> πρὸ τούτου, in preference to this.
> πρὸ τοῦ, before this.

(c) *Dative.*—ἐν, 'in, among (of place or time)':

> ἐν ὀργῇ, ἐν αἰτίᾳ ἔχειν +Accusative.
> To be angry with, to blame.
> ἐν ἐλπίδι εἶναι.
> To hope (and other such phrases).
> ἐν τῷ ἐμφανεῖ.
> Openly.
> ἐν τῷ παραυτίκα.
> Immediately (and similar phrases).
> ἐν τοῖς πρῶτοι.
> The very first.
> ἐν ὀφθαλμοῖς ἔχειν.
> To have before one's eyes.

σύν (ξύν), 'with':

> σὺν (τοῖς) θεοῖς, with the help of the gods.

GREEK PROSE USAGE

It is used in enumerating *things* that form a total:

σὺν θείῳ καὶ πίσσῃ, together with brimstone and tar.

μετά with genitive is used for *persons* (q.v.). Thucydides uses ξύν for persons:

ξὺν γυναιξὶ καὶ παισίν.
With (including) the women and children.

Also:

ξὺν φόβῳ, ξὺν ἀνάγκῃ, with fear, with necessity.

NOTE.—The opposite of σύν is χωρίς, 'apart from, besides':

χωρὶς τῆς ἄλλης προσόδου, apart from the other revenue.

χωρίς is used as an adverb, 'besides'.

The opposite of μετά, 'with', is usually ἄνευ, 'without':

ἄνευ εὐψυχίας, without courage.
ἄνευ τοῦ δήμου, without the consent of the people.

(2) PREPOSITIONS WITH TWO CASES

διά (i) with accusative, 'on account of, owing to' (denoting not only motive but also purpose):

διὰ τοῦτο, on account of this or for this purpose.
δι' ἀχθηδόνα, to cause annoyance.
δι' ἐμέ, owing to me.

(ii) With genitive, 'through (of place or time), by means of':

δι' ὀλίγου, quickly or at a short distance.
διὰ παντός, throughout.
διὰ τάχους, with speed.
διὰ φιλίας ἰέναι, to be friendly with (with dative).

κατά (i) with accusative, 'down, along, according to, by (distributive)':

κατὰ μικρόν, a small part (cf. ἐπὶ πολύ).
καθ' ἡμέραν, daily.
κατὰ νόμον, lawfully.
κατὰ πόλεις, by cities.

> καθ' ἡσυχίαν, at leisure.
> κατὰ χώραν, on the spot.
> κατ' οἶκον, at home.
> κατὰ μόνας (sc. δυνάμεις), unaided.
> ὅσον καθ' ἕνα ἄνδρα, as far as one man could.
> καθ' ἕκαστον, individually.
> τὰ κατὰ τὰς σπονδάς, the terms of the truce.

(ii) With genitive, 'down from, against':

> κατὰ τῆς πέτρας, down from the rock.
> κατὰ πάντων, against all.

μετά (i) with accusative, 'after':

> μετὰ τὸν πόλεμον, after the war.

(ii) With genitive, 'with':

> μετ' αὐτοῦ, with him.
> μετ' ἀληθείας, with truth, correctly.

ὑπέρ (i) with accusative, 'over, beyond, past':

> ὑπὲρ δύναμιν, beyond one's power.
> βαδίζων ὑπὲρ τὰς Πύλας, making his way past Thermopylae.

(ii) With genitive, 'above, on behalf of, concerning':

> ὑπὲρ τοῦ ἀποτειχίσματος, above the fortification.
> ὑπὲρ τῆς πόλεως, on behalf of the city.
> ὑπὲρ τῆς γραφῆς, about the indictment.

NOTE.—ὑπέρ is often synonymous with περί ('about').

(3) PREPOSITIONS WITH THREE CASES

ἀμφί (i) with accusative, 'about' (of place, time, number):

> ἀμφὶ δείλην, towards evening.
> οἱ ἀμφὶ Πλάτωνα, Plato and his followers.
> ἀμφί τι ἔχειν (εἶναι), to be busied about something.

(ii) With genitive
(iii) With dative } rare in prose.

GREEK PROSE USAGE

ἐπί (i) with accusative, 'towards, against, for, after, on to':

> ἐπὶ τὸν ἵππον ἀναβῆναι, to mount a horse.
> ἐφ' ὕδωρ ἰέναι, to go for water.
> ἐπὶ τοὺς πολεμίους, against the enemy.
> ἐπ' αὐτὸ τοῦτο, for this very purpose.
> ἐπὶ πολύ, widely.
> ὡς ἐπὶ τὸ πολύ, for the most part.

NOTE.—ἐπὶ πολύ is used as one word with the genitive:

> ἐπὶ πολὺ τῆς χώρας, a large part of the country.
> ἐπὶ πολὺ τῆς ἡμέρας, for a great part of the day.

(ii) With genitive, ' on, in the time of, in charge of, in the direction of':

> ἐπ' ἀγκύρας ὁρμεῖν, to lie at anchor.
> ἐπ' οἴκου, homewards.
> οἱ ἐφ' ἡμῶν, men of our time.
> οἱ ἐπὶ τῶν πραγμάτων, those in charge of affairs.
> ἐπὶ τεττάρων, four deep.
> ἐπὶ πολλῶν, on many occasions.
> ἐπὶ τῶν νεῶν, on the ships.
> μένειν ἐπί + genitive, to abide in, persevere in.

NOTE.—ἐπί + dative for 'on' is uncommon except with names of places and ἐπὶ θαλάσσῃ, 'on the sea, by the sea'.

(iii) With dative, 'after, on condition, in addition to, in the power of, for the purpose of':

> ἐπὶ τούτοις, thereupon.
> ἐπὶ μισθῷ, for pay.
> ἐπὶ τῇ ἴσῃ καὶ ὁμοίᾳ, on fair and equal terms.
> τὰ ἐφ' ἡμῖν, what is in our power.
> ἐπὶ τῷ παρόντι.
> Under the present circumstances.
> ἐπὶ προφάσει.
> On a pretext.
> ἐπ' ὠφελίᾳ τῶν ἀδικουμένων.
> For the help of the injured (frequently used thus for a purpose clause).

ἐπ' ἐλευθερίᾳ.
On condition of freedom, cf. ἐφ' ᾧ, on condition that.

ὡς ἐπὶ μεγέθει.
Considering the size.

ἐπὶ τοῖς ἄλλοις.
In addition to the others.

παρά (i) with accusative; 'to, near, beside, contrary to, compared with, beyond':

>παρὰ τοὺς φίλους φοιτᾶν.
>To visit one's friends.
>
>παρὰ νόμον, παρὰ δόξαν.
>Unlawfully, unexpectedly (and the like).
>
>παρὰ τοὺς ἄλλους.
>In comparison with the rest.
>
>παρ' οὐδὲν ποιεῖσθαι.
>To make of no account.
>
>παρ' οὐδέν, παρὰ μικρὸν ἦλθον (with infinitive).
>I was within a little of . . .
>
>παρὰ γῆν πλεῖν.
>To sail along the coast.
>
>παρὰ πολύ.
>By far.
>
>παρ' αὐτὰ τὰ συμβάντα.
>At the actual time of the events.

NOTE.—παρά with accusative meaning 'to' with verbs of motion is used only of persons:

>ἔπλευσαν παρ' αὐτούς, they sailed to join them.

(ii) With genitive, 'from (of persons)':

>μανθάνειν παρά τινος, to learn from someone.
>δίκην λαβεῖν παρά τινος, to punish someone.

(iii) With dative, 'at, beside (of persons)':

>παρὰ σοί, with you.
>παρ' ὑμῖν, among you.

περί (i) with accusative, 'about, near':

>περὶ μέσας νύκτας, about midnight.
>σπουδάζειν περί τι, to be busied about something.

περὶ τούτους τοὺς χώρους, around these places.
περὶ τὸν τάφον, connected with the burial.

(ii) With genitive, 'about, concerning':

τὰ περὶ τῆς δίκης.
The facts of the case.

περὶ ἴσου.
For an equal prize (also ὑπὲρ τῶν ἴσων).

περὶ τῶν ἐσχάτων κινδυνεύειν.
To run mortal danger.

περὶ πολλοῦ, ὀλίγου, οὐδενός, παντός, πλείστου ποιεῖσθαι.
To count of much, little, no, all, very much importance.

(iii) With dative, 'about, concerning', chiefly poetic, but Thucydides has:

περὶ ταῖς ναυσὶ φοβεῖσθαι, to fear for the ships.

πρός (i) with accusative, 'to, towards, with a view to, according to':

τὰ πρὸς βορέαν.
The northern parts.

πρὸς ταῦτα.
Consequently.

πρὸς βίαν.
Violently (and the like).

πρὸς πόλεμον παρασκευάζεσθαι.
To make preparations with a view to war.

πράττειν πρός τινα.
To negotiate with somebody.

ὀλίγοι πρὸς πολλούς.
Few against many.

πρὸς τὰ παρόντα.
With reference to the present.

(ii) With genitive, 'over against, from, by':

τὰ πρὸς νότου.
From the south.

πρὸς θεῶν.
By the gods.

πρὸς τῶν πολεμίων εἶναι.
To be to the advantage of the enemy.

(iii) With dative, 'at, in addition to':

πρὸς τούτοις, in addition to this.
πρὸς τῇ γῇ, near the land.

NOTE.—

πρὸς δέ, and besides.

ὑπό (i) with accusative, 'under, near (of time)':

ὑπὸ τὴν νύκτα, about nightfall.
τὸ ὑπὸ τὴν ἀκρόπολιν, the part under the Acropolis.

(ii) With genitive, 'under, by (agent), through (cause)':

τὰ ὑπὸ τῆς γῆς, things under the earth.
ὑπὸ τοῦ δήμου, by the people.
ὑφ' ἡδονῆς, through pleasure.

NOTE.—ὑπό is used with things, as well as people:

ὑπὸ τοῦ κακοῦ νικώμενοι, overcome by the disaster.
ὑπὸ ξυμφορῶν πιεζόμενοι, hard pressed by disasters.

Thus used, it is confined to things associated with people, *e.g.* emotions, words, laws, dangers. The instrumental dative is always possible as an alternative. So also:

ὑπὸ χειμῶνος ταλαιπωρεῖν.
To be in distress through the winter.

ἄπορον ποιεῖν ὑπὸ τοῦ ὕδατος.
To make it impossible owing to the water.

(iii) With dative, 'under':

ὑπὸ Συρακοσίοις γίγνεσθαι.
To be at the mercy of the Syracusans.

OTHER PREPOSITIONS

ἄνευ with genitive, 'without, apart from' (see σύν).

ἄχρι, μέχρι with genitive, 'until, as far as':

μέχρι ὀψέ, till late.
μέχρι τῆς τήμερον ἡμέρας, until to-day.
μέχρι τοῦ, up to a certain point, only for a while.

GREEK PROSE USAGE

μεταξύ with genitive, 'between'.

ἕνεκα with genitive, 'on account of, for the sake of' (often put after its noun):

> ἕνεκά γε ψηφισμάτων, as far as decrees are concerned.

πλήν with genitive, 'except'.

ὡς with accusative, 'to (of persons)':

> πρέσβεις ἔπεμψεν ὡς βασιλέα.
> He sent envoys to the great king.

NOTES.—(i) πάρα is used for πάρεστι, ἔνι for ἔνεστι.

(ii) There is a so-called pregnant use of prepositions:

> ἡ ναυμαχία ἐτελεύτα ἐς νύκτα.
> The sea-fight ended at (went on until) night.
>
> ὁ ἐκ Βυζαντίου ἁρμοστὴς μέλλει ἥξειν.
> The governor *in* Byzantium will come.

So:

> ἐκ τοῦ παρεληλυθότος χρόνου, *in* time past.
> ἐκ δεξιᾶς, on the right.
> ἐκ τοῦ ὄπισθεν, in the rear.

(iii) Adverbs of place are used as prepositions with the genitive; such are:

εἴσω, ἐντός, within. ἐγγύς, πέλας, πλησίον, near.
ἔξω, ἐκτός, outside. πόρρω, πρόσω, far from.
ὄπισθεν, behind. εὐθύ, straight towards.
ἀμφοτέρωθεν, on both sides of.

So also:

> λάθρᾳ, κρύφα, secretly, without the knowledge of.

(iv) Connecting particles, like γε, μέν, δέ, γάρ, οὖν, can stand between a preposition and its noun:

> ἐν μὲν τοίνυν τοῖς πρὸς τὴν πόλιν τοιοῦτος.
> Such then is he in public affairs.

THE VERB

1. THE VOICES

(a) The *Active Voice* is, as in English, that in which the subject is represented as acting. Both transitive and intransitive verbs are found in the active, and, as in English, in some verbs the active form is both transitive and intransitive, *e.g. ἐλαύνω*, 'I drive', *τελευτάω*, 'I finish' or 'I die', *ἀνίημι*, 'I cease'.

Some transitive verbs have certain tenses in the active with intransitive meaning, *e.g. ἵστημι*, 'I place', *ἔστην*, 'I stood'. There are also deponents, of middle or passive form, which are active and transitive in meaning.

(b) The *Passive Voice* is, as in English, that in which the subject is represented as acted upon. Verbs which in the active govern an indirect object in the genitive or dative may have that indirect object as the subject in the passive, *e.g. πιστεύεται*, 'he is trusted'.

Some intransitive verbs in the active are used as passives of other verbs, and often take an agent with *ὑπό*. Such are:

ACTIVE	PASSIVE
εὖ ποιέω, I treat well.	εὖ πάσχω, I am well treated.
εὖ λέγω, I speak well of.	εὖ ἀκούω, I am well spoken of.
ἀπολύω, I acquit.	ἀποφεύγω, I am acquitted.
ἐκβάλλω, I cast out.	ἐκπίπτω, I am cast out.
ἀποκτείνω, I kill.	ἀποθνήσκω, I am killed.
διώκω, I prosecute.	φεύγω, I am prosecuted.
κατάγω, I restore.	κατέρχομαι, I am restored.
διδάσκω, I teach.	μανθάνω, I am taught.

(c) The *Middle Voice* is that in which the subject is represented as acting upon himself or in reference to himself.

(i) As reflexive, e.g. λούομαι, 'I bathe', τρέπομαι, 'I turn myself to'.
But the active is used with the reflexive pronoun when the meaning is *expressly* reflexive, e.g. ἀποκτείνειν ἑαυτόν, 'to kill oneself'.

(ii) As causative (with direct object), e.g. διδάσκομαι, 'I have someone taught'.

(iii) With a special meaning, e.g. ἀποδίδομαι, 'I sell'.

(iv) As deponent, e.g. γίγνομαι, 'I become'.

NOTES.—(i) The following aorists are noteworthy:

ὁρμάομαι, I start.	ὡρμήθην.
φαίνομαι, I appear.	ἐφάνην.
φοβοῦμαι, I fear.	ἐφοβήθην.
πείθομαι, I obey.	ἐπείσθην (+ *dative*).
κτάομαι, I acquire.	ἐκτησάμην, I acquired.
	ἐκτήθην, I was acquired.
αἰτιάομαι, I accuse.	ᾐτιασάμην, I accused.
	ᾐτιάθην, I was accused.
δέομαι, I ask.	ἐδεήθην.
οἴομαι, I think.	ᾠήθην.
διαλέγομαι, I converse.	διελέχθην.
πειράομαι, I try.	ἐπειράθην (and ἐπειρασάμην in Thucydides).
αὐλίζομαι, I encamp.	ηὐλισάμην (in Thucydides).
	ηὐλίσθην (in Xenophon).
πορεύομαι, I set out.	ἐπορεύθην.

(ii) The passive of some verbs is used as the passive of the active and middle, e.g.—*Active*: αἱρεῖν, 'to take'; *Middle*: αἱρεῖσθαι, 'to choose'; *Passive*: αἱρεῖσθαι, 'to be taken or chosen'. But ἁλίσκομαι is used of persons ('I am taken').

(iii) The middle of ποιῶ (ποιοῦμαι) is much used with a noun as periphrasis for a verb, e.g.:

> ἀποχώρησιν ποιεῖσθαι, to retreat.
> ἁρπαγὴν ποιεῖσθαι, to plunder.
> γνώμην ποιεῖσθαι, to propose.

ἔκπλουν ποιεῖσθαι, to sail out.
ἐπιμέλειαν ποιεῖσθαι, to care.
ἐπιχείρησιν ποιεῖσθαι, to attempt.
κατάφευξιν ποιεῖσθαι, to take refuge.
κήρυγμα ποιεῖσθαι, to proclaim.
ναυμαχίαν ποιεῖσθαι, to fight a sea-battle.
πέμψιν ποιεῖσθαι, to send.
πλοῦν ποιεῖσθαι, to sail.
πόλεμον ποιεῖσθαι, to make war.
τροπὴν ποιεῖσθαι, to rout.

The passive of ποιοῦμαι is γίγνομαι, used with many military words, e.g. δίωξις, 'pursuit', ἐμβολή, 'attack', ναυμαχία, 'sea-battle', ὁμολογία, 'agreement', στρατεία, 'expedition'; also πάθος, 'disaster', ἁμάρτημα, 'mistake', ὠφελία, 'help'.

(iv) The *Future Middle* of some verbs is used with passive meaning, e.g.:

ἀδικέω, wrong.   ἀδικήσομαι, I shall be wronged.
ἀποστερέω, deprive.   ἀποστερήσομαι, I shall be deprived.
ζημιόω, harm.   ζημιώσεται, harm will be done.
ὠφελέω, help.   ὠφελήσομαι, I shall be helped.

The passive forms, ἀδικηθήσομαι, etc., are also found.

2. THE MOODS

(a) The *Indicative* is used to express simple assertions and questions involving simple assertions. See Oratio Recta.

(b) The *Imperative* is used to express commands. See Oratio Recta.

(c) The *Subjunctive* and *Optative* are used in main and subordinate clauses.

(d) The *Infinitive*, the *Participle* and the *Verbal Adjectives* are called parts of the infinitive mood. For their uses see under separate headings.

3. THE TENSES

A. OF THE INDICATIVE

(a) *Present*, expressing an action going on in present time.

NOTES.—(i) With πάλαι and expressions like πολλὰ ἤδη ἔτη, the present means 'I have long been doing something'.

(ii) In narrative the present often has a historic force, equal to the aorist.

(iii) The present may mean 'I am trying to', *e.g.* πείθω, δίδωμι ('I offer').

(iv) ἥκω, 'I am come', οἴχομαι, 'I am gone', have the force of perfects.

(v) εἶμι, 'I am going', ἰέναι and ἰών (from ἔρχομαι) have present and future significance. The subjunctive, optative and infinitive have future meaning in oratio obliqua.

(b) *Future*, expressing a future action or a future state.

NOTES.—(i) μέλλω with present or future infinitive denotes intention or expectation (also imperfect ἤμελλον): εἰ μέλλω, 'if I am to', ὁ μέλλων, 'he that would'.

(ii) The 2nd person future may express a command (*q.v.*).

(c) *Perfect*, expressing an action already finished in present time, *e.g.* τέθνηκεν, 'he is dead'. The perfect participle with εἰμί is sometimes used.

NOTES.—(i) Perfects with present meaning:

δέδοικα, I fear.
ἐγρήγορα, I am awake.
εἴωθα, I am accustomed.
ἔοικα, I seem.
ἕστηκα, I stand.
κέκτημαι, I possess.
κέκλημαι, I am called.

οἶδα, I know.
πέφυκα, I am.
μέμνημαι, I remember.
γέγονα, I am.
κέκχρημαι, I experience.
τέθραμμαι, I am brought up.

(ii) The pluperfects of these verbs have an imperfect meaning.

(iii) The epistolary perfect :

ἀπέσταλκά σοι τόνδε τὸν λόγον, I send you this speech.

(d) *Future Perfect*, denoting the permanence of the results of an action in future time :

τοῦτο λέγεται καὶ λελέξεται, this is said and will remain said.
ἑστήξω, I shall remain standing.

The above tenses (a), (b), (c), (d) are called primary.

(e) *Imperfect*, expressing an action going on in past time.

NOTES.—(i) With πάλαι and the like, the imperfect means 'I had been doing' :

τὸ Ῥήγιον ἐπὶ πολὺν χρόνον ἐστασίαζεν.
Rhegium had for long been in revolt.

(ii) The imperfect is used for customary or repeated action, sometimes with ἄν (iterative) :

ἐπεκελεύοντο τῷ Νικίᾳ, they kept calling on Nicias.

(iii) It expresses intention and likelihood :

ἠπείγοντο, they were for pushing on.

(iv) It expresses attempted action (as also the present) :

ἐδίδου, he offered.
ἔπειθον, they tried to persuade.

(v) It expresses 'a fact which is either the result of a discussion or just recognized as a fact previously denied, overlooked or misunderstood' :

οὐκ ἦν σοφὸς ὁ ταῦτα εἰπών.
He is not after all wise . . . (as we once thought).

Often with ἄρα.

(vi) It is used (often in Thucydides) for the aorist, especially of πέμπω, κελεύω, δέομαι, ἐθέλω, λέγω and verbs of going (where time is needed for the completion of the action):

> οἱ Κερκυραῖοι ἔπεμπον τὴν ὠφελίαν ἅσμενοι.
> The Corcyreans sent the help gladly.

(vii) It expresses uncompleted action:

> ἐπειδὴ οὐ ξυνεχώρουν . . .
> Since they were not likely to yield.

(f) *Aorist*, expressing the momentary occurrence of an action in past time; it is the tense of narrative.

NOTES.—(i) The ingressive aorist denotes entrance into a state or condition (aorist of first attainment):

> ἐβασίλευσεν.
> He became king.
>
> οἱ Λακεδαιμόνιοι ἡγήσαντο τῶν ξυμπολεμησάντων Ἑλλήνων.
> The Spartans *assumed the leadership* of the Greeks who *entered the war* as allies.

This use is generally with 1st aorists, but ᾔσθοντο means 'they became aware'.

(ii) The complexive aorist expresses a series of repetitions collectively — a continued action viewed as a simple event in past time:

> ἐβασίλευσε, he reigned (ἐβασίλευε, he continued to reign).
> ἐπολέμησαν, they waged war.

(iii) The aorist is used for the pluperfect, regularly in sentences introduced by 'when, since, until,' often in relative and other subordinate clauses, occasionally in main clauses:

> οὐκ ἐτόλμησαν . . . πρὶν συνέλαβον.
> They did not dare . . . until they had seized.
>
> ταῦτα μέγιστα διεφάνη.
> It had become clear that these were the greatest.

(iv) The gnomic aorist expresses a general truth (what is customary):

> πολλάκις τὸ ἔλασσον πλῆθος ἠμύνατο τοὺς πλέονας.
> Often the smaller number resists the larger.

This use is also found where in English the perfect tense with 'have' is used more commonly than the present (in particular with πολλάκις, ἤδη or οὔπω):

> πολλάκις ἐθαύμασα, I have often wondered.
> οὔπω εἶδόν ποτε, never yet have I seen.

(v) The timeless aorist, in participles, denotes merely the act, not time anterior to the main verb:

> ὡμολόγησαν Ἀθηναίοις, τεῖχος καθελόντες καὶ ναῦς παραδόντες.
> They came to terms with the Athenians, pulling down the wall and handing over their ships.

It is used with the aorists of τυγχάνω, λανθάνω and φθάνω; also the future, e.g.:

> ἐλάθομεν ἐπιπεσόντες, we attacked them unawares.
> λήσομεν ἐπιπεσόντες, we shall attack them unawares.

See also Uses of the Participles.

(vi) The epistolary aorist:

> μετ' Ἀρταβάζου, ὅν σοι ἔπεμψα, πράττε.
> Act with Artabazus, whom I am sending you.

(g) *The Pluperfect*, expressing an action finished at some time in the past:

> οἱ μὲν δὴ ἐν τῇ Πλαταίᾳ οὕτως ἐπεπράγεσαν.
> Those in Plataea had fared thus.

NOTES.—(i) The perfect participle with ἦν is sometimes used.

(ii) Of verbs whose perfect has a present meaning, the pluperfect has an imperfect meaning, e.g. ᾔδη, 'I knew'. The above tenses (e), (f), (g) are called historic.

B. THE TENSES OF THE IMPERATIVE (See Direct Command)

(a) *Present*, expressing a continued or repeated action:

> μὴ νομίζετε, do not believe.

(b) *Aorist*, expressing a momentary or single action:

> εἰπέ μοι, tell me.

GREEK PROSE USAGE

C. Tenses of the Subjunctive

(a) *Present,* expressing a continued or repeated action.
(b) *Aorist,* expressing a single or momentary action.

NOTE.—The distinction of *time* which marks the present and aorist in the indicative disappears in the subjunctive, but in temporal, relative and conditional clauses requiring ἄν + subjunctive, the aorist subjunctive may refer, as shown by the context, to a time preceding that of the main verb, and so acquire the force of the English perfect or future perfect, while the present subjunctive refers to an action continuing through the time of the main verb:

ὅταν τιθῆσθε τοὺς νόμους . . .
Whenever you are enacting laws (All the time that . . .).

ἐπειδὰν θῆσθε τοὺς νόμους . . .
Whenever you have enacted laws.

D. Tenses of the Optative (when not in oratio obliqua)

(a) *Present,* expressing a continued or repeated action.
(b) *Aorist,* expressing a single or momentary action:

εἴθε μὴ ταῦτα πάσχοιεν.
May they not (ever) suffer this (habitually).

εἴθε μὴ ταῦτα πάθοιεν.
May they not suffer this (in a single case).

(c) *Future,* used only in oratio obliqua in historic sequence, to represent a future indicative of oratio recta:

ἀποκρινάμενοι ὅτι πέμψοιεν (πέμψουσιν).
Answering that they would send.

In oratio obliqua (*q.v.*) the optative represents the indicative or subjunctive (in the same tense) of the oratio recta in historic sequence.

E. Tenses of the Infinitive (for oratio obliqua see below)

(a) *Present,* expressing continued or repeated action.

NOTE.—With δεῖ and χρή, the past sense is expressed by the main verb ; the infinitive is present, *e.g.* :

τί ἔδει με ποιεῖν; What ought I to have done ?

(*b*) *Future*, expressing futurity.

NOTE.—The future (occasionally present) infinitive is used with verbs of hoping, promising, swearing :

ὤμοσαν ἦ μὴν βοηθήσειν, they swore to help.

Also with other verbs, to mark an impending action :

διενοοῦντο κλήσειν, they intended to blockade.

With verbs of hoping, the potential aorist infinitive with ἄν is used (and sometimes the simple aorist infinitive). See also Indirect Statement.

(*c*) *Aorist*, expressing a momentary or single action. The distinction between present and aorist infinitives is shown thus :

ἐδέοντο τῶν Κερκυραίων μὴ περιορᾶν (present continuous) . . .
ἀλλὰ καταλῦσαι τὸν πόλεμον (aorist single).

They asked the Corcyreans not to allow . . . but to end the war.

NOTES.—(i) This distinction is not always observed, the aorist being used for present after an aorist main verb.

(ii) When the infinitive has the article, the aorist has usually a past time significance.

In Oratio Obliqua (*q.v.*), the present, future and perfect infinitives are used in primary and historic sequence for the corresponding tenses of the indicative in direct speech. The aorist infinitive is used with aorist meaning : in historic sequence it translates the English pluperfect :

ἐλέγετο δοῦναι { He was said to have given.
It was said that he had given.

NOTES.—(i) The present infinitive may have an imperfect meaning in primary sequence :

Λακεδαιμονίους φασὶν ἐθέλειν.
They say the Spartans were willing.

(ii) The moods of εἶμι (*ibo*) are usually present in meaning, *except in oratio obliqua*.

In conditional sentences in Oratio Obliqua (*q.v.*) :

(i) present infinitive with ἄν stands for the imperfect indicative and present optative with ἄν.

(ii) The aorist infinitive with ἄν stands for the aorist indicative and aorist optative with ἄν.

(iii) Both present and aorist infinitives with ἄν stand for the potential optative with ἄν, present for continued action, aorist for single action, *e.g.* :

> ἐνόμιζον ἅπασαν ἂν ἔχειν Πελοπόννησον.
> They thought they would hold all the Peloponnese.
>
> ὑμᾶς ἂν ἑλέσθαι νομίζω.
> I think you would choose.

NOTE.—The ἄν is often attached to the governing verb, *e.g.* :

> οὐκ ἄν μοι δοκῶ, I don't think I could.

F. TENSES OF THE PARTICIPLE (except in Oratio Obliqua, *q.v.*)

(*a*) *Present*, expressing a continued or repeated action, contemporary with that of the main verb.

NOTES.—(i) With νῦν it is *absolutely* present, *e.g.* :

> τὴν νῦν Βοιωτίαν καλουμένην ᾤκησαν.
> They inhabited what *is now* called Boeotia.

(ii) It may have an imperfect meaning, *e.g.* :

> οἱ παρόντες καταμαρτυρήσουσιν.
> Those who were present will testify.

(*b*) *Future*, expressing an action future in time to the main verb. See also Uses of the Participles.

(*c*) *Aorist*, expressing a momentary or single action, which is past with reference to the time of the main verb. It thus translates 'having done' (ποιήσας).

NOTES.—(i) With λανθάνω, τυγχάνω, φθάνω the aorist participle coincides with the verb in time, *e.g.* :

> ἔλαθον ἀπελθόντες, they went away unobserved.

So even with reference to the future :

βουλοίμην ἂν λαθεῖν αὐτὸν ἀπελθών.
I should like to get away unnoticed by him.

(ii) If with these verbs a reference to the past is needed, the perfect participle is used.

(iii) The present participle with these verbs expresses a continued action or state. See also p. 64 (xii).

THE VERBAL ADJECTIVE IN -τέος

(1) It is formed from the verb stem (which is generally the same as in the weak aorist passive), *e.g.* :

> λύω (ἐλύθην) : λυτέος.
> πείθω (ἐπείσθην) : πειστέος.

(2) To translate 'must', this verbal adjective is used impersonally in the neuter singular or plural with ἐστι expressed or understood : it may govern an object, direct or indirect, in the case governed by the verb from which it is derived, and the agent is put in the dative, *e.g.* :

> κολαστέον (κολαστέα) ἐστὶ τὸν παῖδα ἡμῖν.
> We must punish the boy.
>
> ἐπιχειρητέον ἐστὶ τῷ ἔργῳ ἡμῖν.
> We must set about the work.
>
> πιστὰ καὶ ὁμήρους δοτέον καὶ ληπτέον.
> Pledges and hostages must be given and received.

If the verb governs a direct object, the verbal adjective can be used personally, *e.g.* :

> ὁ παῖς κολαστέος ἐστὶν ἡμῖν, the boy is to be punished by us.

NOTES.—(i) Even with transitive verbs the personal construction is less common.

(ii) Verbs used in the active and middle with different meanings have the verbal adjective used impersonally, *e.g.* :

> πειστέον, one must persuade or one must obey.

(iii) The verbal adjective is found in the genitive plural :

> περὶ τῶν ὑμῖν πρακτέων, about what you must do.

(iv) The accusative and infinitive with δεῖ is an equivalent translation of 'must'.

(v) When 'must' means not compulsion but a degree of certainty, use ἄρα, e.g.:

ἔκφρων ἄρ' ἦν ὁ ἄνθρωπος, the man must have been mad.

(vi) There is another verbal adjective in -τός, which usually expresses capability, e.g.:

> ἀκουστός, capable of being heard.
> πρακτός, practicable.

(vii) Both verbal adjectives are *passive* in meaning.

THE NEGATIVE

GENERALLY speaking, οὐ, οὐδέ, οὔτε, οὐδείς, οὐδαμῶς, etc., are used in main clauses (statements or questions) in the indicative and in the optative with ἄν.

μή, μηδέ, μήτε, μηδείς, μηδαμῶς, etc., are used for negative conceptions, e.g. a wish, purpose, condition.

(1) In indirect statements with ὅτι or ὡς the negative is οὐ. In the accusative (nominative) and infinitive or participle construction the negative is οὐ. But if the verb of saying or thinking is in a construction requiring the negative μή (e.g. the imperative, or after ἐάν, εἰ), then the negative is μή in the accusative and infinitive, e.g.:

> νόμιζε μηδὲν εἶναι βέβαιον.
> Consider that nothing is definite.
>
> ἐπειδὰν ἴδητε μηδὲν ὑμῖν ἔνον . . .
> When you see that you can do nothing . . .

So with a verb expressing 'confident belief impressed on others', the negative is generally μή:

> εὖ ἴσμεν μὴ ἂν ὑμᾶς ἧσσον λυπηροὺς γενομένους.
> We are sure that you would not have been less oppressive.
>
> νομίσαντες μὴ ἂν ἱκανοὶ γενέσθαι.
> Being sure that they would not be able.

(2) In indirect questions, οὐ is used: after εἰ, 'if, whether', both οὐ and μή are found. 'Or not' is ἢ οὐ or ἢ μή. (See Indirect Questions.)

(3) In indirect commands the negative is μή.

(4) With all uses of the infinitive (except indirect statement) the negative is μή:

> ἔδοξεν αὐτοῖς μὴ κινεῖν τοὺς στρατιώτας.
> They decided not to move the soldiers.

But if the negative from the governing verb is repeated with the infinitive, οὐ is kept:

> οὐκ ἐᾷ εἰσιέναι οὐδεμίαν γυναῖκα.
> He allows no woman to enter.

(5) With the participle (except as in (1)) the negative is οὐ, but if the participle is used conditionally or generally, the negative is μή:

> ὄντες καὶ πρὸ τοῦ μὴ ταχεῖς.
> Being the sort of men who were not quick even before this.

So with an adjective:

> αἱ μὴ καλαὶ ἐπιθυμίαι.
> Base desires (such as are not noble).
>
> οὐ γὰρ ἔστιν ἄρχειν μὴ διδόντα μισθόν.
> For it is impossible to command if you do not give pay.

If the clause in which the participle occurs demands the negative μή (*e.g.* the protasis of a condition), μή will be found with the participle irrespective of its use:

> ἀβελτερώτατος ἂν εἴη εἰ ὑμῶν μηδὲν ἐγκαλούντων ἐφ' αὑτὸν προείποι τρέπεσθαι.
> He would be most foolish if, while you make no complaint, he should warn you to turn against him.

(6) The negative μή is used in main clauses in direct commands, deliberative questions and wishes.

(7) The negative μή is used in subordinate clauses:

   (i) Final clauses.
  (ii) After verbs of fearing.
 (iii) In the protasis of conditional sentences.
 (iv) Temporal clauses with ἄν + subjunctive or with optative.
  (v) Indefinite relative clauses.
 (vi) After verbs of precaution.

(8) οὐ μή is used with the future indicative or aorist subjunctive to express a strong prohibition or an emphatic negation (see Commands).

(9) The *Repeated Negative*.

(a) A simple negative (οὐ or μή) is cancelled by a foregoing negative :

οὐδὲ τὸν Φορμίωνα οὐχ ὁρᾷ, he sees Phormio very well.

(b) A compound negative following a simple or compound negative emphasizes it :

οὐδεὶς εἰς οὐδὲν οὐδέποτ' ἂν γένοιτο ἄξιος.
No one would ever be fit for anything.

(10) The negative usually precedes a preposition, *e.g.* :

οὐχ ὑπ' ἀξίων, by unworthy men.

But :

ἐν οὐ πολλῷ, in a short time.

(11) ὅσον οὐ = 'all but' (μόνον οὐ) :

ὅσον οὐκ ἔμελλον ἀνάγεσθαι.
They were all but on the point of putting out to sea.

ὅτι μή = 'except' :

οὐ γὰρ ἦν κρήνη ὅτι μὴ μία, for there was no well except one.

ὅσα μή = 'except in so far as, provided only . . . not' (with participle) :

τῆς γῆς ἐκράτουν ὅσα μὴ προϊόντες πολὺ ἐκ τῶν ὅπλων.
There were masters of the land, provided they did not advance far from camp.

NOTES ON SOME CONJUNCTIONS AND PARTICLES

καί, 'and, even, also'.

(i) It often introduces a sentence, 'and so', 'and in fact':

> καὶ εἴρηται αὐτῆς τὰ μέγιστα.
> And in fact most of it has been said.

(ii) It is corrective, 'or':

> διὰ τὸ ἀντιπάλους καὶ ἔτι πλείους εἶναι.
> Because they are equal, or rather, superior.
>
> ταῦτα καὶ παραπλήσια.
> This or to this effect.

(iii) 'Also', 'even':

> αἱ δὲ καὶ ὤκειλαν, other ships also ran aground.
> καὶ μάλ' ἀκριβῶς οἶδα, I know well enough.

(iv) It expresses closer definition:

> κύριος Πυλῶν καὶ τῶν παρόδων ἐστί.
> He is master of Thermopylae, that is, of the pass ...
>
> οἱ μὲν ἄρχουσι καὶ τυραννοῦσι.
> The (traitors) hold despotic rule.

καὶ ... δέ, 'and indeed, and besides':

> καὶ γράψω δέ, and I will make a proposal besides.

καὶ δὴ καί, 'and in particular':

> ἐν τῷ ἔμπροσθεν ... καὶ δὴ καὶ τότε.
> Formerly ... and in particular on that occasion.

Also ἀτὰρ καί (esp. in Plato):

> καὶ ἄλλοι τινές με ἤδη ἤροντο, ἀτὰρ καὶ Εὐηνὸς πρῴην.
> Others too have already asked me, and in particular Evenus, yesterday.

καὶ γάρ, 'for indeed'.

καὶ δή, 'straightway':

καὶ δὴ πειράσομαι λέγειν, I will try straightway to tell you.

καί τοι, 'and yet'.

ἄλλως τε καί, 'especially'.

ὅμοιος καί, 'similar to' (see Comparison).

Coincidence in time expressed by co-ordinate clauses:

ἅμα ἀκηκόαμέν τι καὶ τριηράρχους καθίσταμεν.
It is only when we have received news that we appoint captains.

NOTE.—A single τε for καί is rare in prose, but see below.

τε . . . καί, 'both . . . and'.

τε is enclitic and is attached to the first of the connected terms:

ἐν τοσαύτῃ ἀγρυπνίᾳ τε καὶ λύπῃ.
In such sleeplessness and grief.

ἀκροάσει τῶν τε ἐν ἀρχῇ ὄντων καὶ τῶν νόμων.
In obedience to those in authority and to the laws.

With a common article or adjective or preposition we may have:

οἵ τε εὐοπλότατοι καὶ εὐειδέστατοι.
The best armed and most beautiful.

ἐν τοσαύτῃ τε ἀγρυπνίᾳ καὶ λύπῃ.
In such sleeplessness and grief

(instead of the order above).

ἄνευ τε δόλου καὶ ἀπάτης.
Without trick or deceit.

It is used of simultaneous occurrence:

ἡμέρα τε σχεδὸν ὑπέφαινε καὶ οἱ ἄρχοντες ἧκον.
Scarcely had day dawned when the leaders arrived.

NOTE.—τε is used as an inferential connective:

προσέβαλόν τε εὐθὺς καὶ ἐς χεῖρας ᾖσαν.
And so they attacked at once and joined battle.

And so they asked them not to build walls but to pull down ...
ἠξίουν τε αὐτοὺς μὴ τειχίζειν ἀλλὰ καὶ καθελεῖν ...

It also sums up the preceding remarks :

συνελών τε λέγω, briefly, then, I say ...

τε ... τε implies two concurrent acts having the same object in view.

ἐκκλησίαν τε οὐκ ἐποίει ... τήν τε πόλιν ἐφύλασσεν.
He did not summon an assembly ... and guarded the city.

καί ... καί, 'both ... and', emphasizes the several co-ordinated members, τε ... καί emphasizes the connection of the members to form a whole.

ἤτοι ... ἤ, 'either ... or', usually emphasizes the first member :

ἤτοι θεοί γε ἢ θεῶν παῖδες.
Either gods or (may be) sons of gods.

οὐδέ, μηδέ, 'and not, nor, not even, not either' :

καὶ οὐδὲ Δία ξένιον ᾐδέσθη.
And he did not even reverence Zeus, god of strangers.
οἶμαι δὲ οὐδὲ ἄλλον οὐδένα.
And I think no one else either.

οὔτε (μήτε) ... οὔτε (μήτε), 'neither ... nor', connecting two negative ideas. A third one takes οὐδέ, μηδέ :

ὃ μοι δοκεῖτε οὔτ' ἐνθυμηθῆναι ... οὔτ' ἐγὼ ἐχρησάμην ... οὐδ' ἂν νῦν ἐχρησάμην ...
A point which I think neither you envisaged, nor did I use it ... nor would I have used it now.

οὔτε (μήτε) ... τε, 'not ... but', used to connect an affirmative idea to a negative :

οὔτ' ἄλλοτε εἱλόμην λέγειν ... νῦν τε πεπαρρησίασμαι.
I did not at other times choose to speak ... but now I have spoken freely.

μήτε προδώσειν ἀλλήλους σύμμαχοί τε ἔσεσθαι.
They promised not to betray one another but to be allies.

GREEK PROSE USAGE

οὐκ . . . οὐδέ, 'not . . . nor even, much less':

ἐκκλησίαν οὐκ ἐποίει οὐδὲ ξύλλογον οὐδένα.
He did not summon an assembly nor even any meeting.

οἱ δὲ οὐ προσεδέξαντο αὐτὸν ἐς τὴν πόλιν οὐδ' ἐπὶ τὸ κοινόν.
But they did not receive him into the city, much less to the assembly.

ἀλλά, 'but', 'expressing adversative connexion by way of correction'. It is also resumptive:

τὰ μὲν ἄλλα σιωπῶ, ἀλλὰ τοσαύτης ἐρημίας ἐπειλημμένοι . . .
The rest I omit, but having obtained such a clear field . . .

It is apodotic:

ἀλλὰ νῦν γε, now at least (if not before).

It is used in rhetorical altercation:

πότερον ταῖς ναυσίν; ἀλλ' ἥσσους ἐσμέν· ἀλλὰ τοῖς χρήμασιν;
Trusting in ships? Nay, we are inferior. In money, then?

It means 'well, . . .', introducing direct speech. ἀλλὰ μήν is transitional, 'and yet'. ἀλλὰ γάρ, 'but the fact is':

ἀλλ' οὐ γὰρ ἐπίσταμαι, but the fact is I do not know.

ἀλλὰ δή, 'but you may object' (at enim). ἀλλ' ἤ, 'except':

ἀλλ' ἢ μὴ φανερῶς γε ἀξιῶν ψηφίζεσθαι.
Except asking them not to vote publicly.

ἀλλ' οὖν . . . γε, 'at the worst' (ἀλλά has no co-ordinating force):

ὅσα ἔπασχον οἱ Ἕλληνες, ἀλλ' οὖν ὑπὸ γνησίων ἠδικοῦντο.
Whatever the Greeks suffered, they were at any rate wronged by genuine sons of Greece.

οὐ μόνον . . . ἀλλὰ καί
οὐχ ὅπως . . . ἀλλά } 'not only . . . but also'.
οὐχ ὅτι, μὴ ὅτι . . . ἀλλὰ (καί)

οὐχ ὅτι, μὴ ὅτι, οὐχ ὅπως . . . ἀλλ' οὐδέ, 'not only not, but not even':

μὴ ὅτι τὰ ἐν τῇ Εὐρώπῃ, ἀλλ' οὐδ' ἐν τῇ Ἀσίᾳ.
Not only not the states in Europe, but not even in Asia.

οὐ (οὐδέ) ... μὴ ὅτι, 'not ..., much less (not to mention)':

οὐδ' ἀναπνεῖν, μὴ ὅτι λέγειν τι δυνησόμεθα.
We shall not be able even to breathe, much less say anything.

δέ, 'and, but', expressing something additional, without correction or contradiction. It is the commonest connecting word.

μέν ... δέ (δέ may be repeated), 'on the one hand .... but on the other', expresses opposition between two or more terms or clauses, e.g.:

λέγεις μὲν εὖ, πράττεις δ' οὐδέν.
You speak well, but do nothing.

NOTES.—(i) It must always be possible to translate δέ by 'and' or 'but', except δέ in apodosis (apodotic):

ἆθλα γὰρ οἷς κεῖται ἀρετῆς μέγιστα, τοῖς δὲ καὶ ἄνδρες ἄριστοι πολιτεύουσι.
For where the prize for valour is greatest, there the citizens are most loyal to their state.

(ii) μέν and δέ are placed after the words opposed; with δέ this word is always first.

They are placed after conjunctions or relatives, when dependent clauses are contrasted, e.g. πρὶν μέν, ἐπεὶ δέ, ἃς μέν, ἃς δέ. With a noun and article they usually come after the article, e.g. ὁ μὲν βασιλεύς ... οἱ δὲ στρατιῶται.

(iii) μέν may be answered by ἔπειτα, ἀλλά, ἀτάρ, εἶτα, without δέ.

(iv) μέν is used without δέ following (= μήν, μέντοι) in clauses beginning with ἀλλά after a negative clause, e.g.:

οὔ τοι δὴ ἀφῖκται, ἀλλὰ δοκεῖ μέν μοι ἥξειν τήμερον.
He has not yet arrived, but I think he will come to-day.

πάνυ μὲν οὖν.
Yes indeed.

(v) μέν does not usually connect, but it is found alone at the beginning of speeches :

οἱ μὲν πολλοὶ τῶν ἐνθάδε εἰρηκότων.
Most of those who have spoken here,

and when it summarizes and dismisses a subject :

τοιούτῳ μὲν πάθει οἱ Ἀθηναῖοι ἐπιέζοντο.
Such then was the disaster under which the Athenians suffered.

οὕτω μὲν Σιτάλκης ξύμμαχος ἐγένετο τοῖς Ἀθηναίοις.
Thus then Sitalces became an ally of the Athenians.

See also δή.

γάρ, 'for'.

(a) *Narrativum*, introducing a narrative (= 'now') :

ἦν γάρ ποτε χρόνος.
Once upon a time.

τοῦ γὰρ Φωκικοῦ συστάντος πολέμου.
Now when the Phocian war broke out . . .

(b) Introducing a clause anticipated by a preceding τοῦτο and the like, or a promised statement :

τοῦτο ἐτόλμησε μαντεύσασθαι· ἤρετο γὰρ δή.
This question he dared to put ; he actually asked.

τεκμήριον δέ· οὔτε γὰρ οἱ Λακεδαιμόνιοι καθ' ἑαυτοὺς στρατεύουσιν . . .
Here is a proof ; the Lacedaemonians do not invade alone . . .

ἐγώ σοι ἐρῶ· τῇ γὰρ ὑστεραίᾳ δεῖ με ἀποθνήσκειν.
I will tell you ; I am to be put to death on the day after . . .

(c) Meaning 'for otherwise' :

δῆλον δέ· τὸ γὰρ ἔρυμα οὐκ ἂν ἐτειχίσαντο.
Obviously, for otherwise they would not have fortified the stronghold.

(d) In answers to questions :

ἱκανῶς ἐν τοῖς ἔμπροσθεν διήλθομεν; ἱκανῶς γάρ.
We have shown sufficiently already ? Yes, sufficiently.

καὶ γάρ, καὶ γάρ τοι, 'for indeed' (in addition to other reasons). καὶ γὰρ οὐδέ, οὐδὲ γάρ =*neque enim*. τοιγαροῦν, 'the result is that . . .'.

ἐπεί, 'when', is used as a co-ordinating conjunction :

> ἐπεὶ τοσόνδε εἰπέ.
> For tell me this much.
> ἐπεὶ καὶ τοῦτό γέ μοι δοκεῖ καλὸν εἶναι.
> And yet this also seems to me to be right.

ἄρα, 'of course, as might have been expected, to be sure' :

> ἐγὼ δὲ οὐδὲν ἄρα τούτων ποιήσω.
> But I shall do none of these things, of course.

It is used, especially with the imperfect, to draw a conclusion, showing the light which the present throws on the past :

> καὶ εἰκότως ἄρα οὐκ ἐγίγνετο.
> And with good reason, as it turned out, it was not so.
> οἱ δ' ἄρα πάντες ἐχώρουν.
> But they, as it turned out, all advanced.

In conditions :

> εἴ τι ἄρα μὴ προχωροίη.
> In the unlikely event that something went amiss.

εἰ μὴ ἄρα, 'unless perchance' (ironical = *nisi forte*).

γε, 'indeed, at least, at any rate' :

> ἔγωγε.
> I for my part.
> καὶ ταῦτά γε.
> Ay, and that too . . .
> φασί γέ τοι δὴ οἱ τούτων κύριοι.
> Those in charge of these matters say so, at any rate.

It is used to cap a previous statement by the speaker or an opponent = 'yes, and ; yes, but' :

> ἢν δέ γε οἶμαί ποτε ἄλλος πόλεμος καταλάβῃ.
> Yes, and I suppose if ever another war befall them.
> ἐπὶ τὴν ἡμετέραν χώραν ἔρχεσθε. οὐ κακῶς γε ποιήσοντες.
> You are coming to invade our land. Yes, but with no harmful intent.

When placed between the article and participle it emphasizes the participle :

> τοῖς γε μετασχοῦσι τῶν κινδύνων.
> To those who at least shared the dangers.
>
> τά γ' ἐμοὶ δοκοῦντα.
> My own humble opinion.

ἀλλὰ μήν . . . γε, καί . . . γε, οὐδέ γε, emphasizing a fresh point.

γε δή :

> πρίν γε δὴ οἱ Συρακόσιοι ἔτρεψαν τοὺς Ἀθηναίους.
> Until the decisive moment when the Syracusans routed the Athenians.

ὅς γε = *quippe qui* :

> ὡς δὲ ἐχθροὶ πάντες ἴστε οἵ γε ἦλθον.
> That they are enemies you all know, since they came.

NOTE.—γε must not be used as equivalent to δή.

δή, 'then, indeed, certainly' :

> ἐν δὲ δὴ τοῖς πολεμικοῖς.
> In operations of war, certainly.
>
> οὐ μὲν δὴ τοῦτό γε ἐρῶ.
> I am certainly not going to say this.
>
> τότε δή.
> Then and not till then.
>
> καὶ τότε δὴ ἔδοσαν τὴν σκυτάλην ἐκείνῳ.
> And then they gave the staff to him.

It gives the result of facts just stated :

> οὕτω δὴ οὐκ εἰδότες . . ., so then in ignorance . . .

It dismisses a subject :

> οἱ μὲν δὴ ἐν τῇ Πλαταίᾳ οὕτως ἐπεπράγεσαν.
> Those in Plataea, then, had fared thus.

It is used ironically :

> δεδιὼς μὴ διαφθαρῇ δὴ ὑπ' Ἀλκιβιάδου.
> Fearing lest he be ruined forsooth by Alcibiades.

It is used in the apodosis to ἐπεί :

> ἐπεὶ δὲ ἀφίκοντο . . . ἐδόκει δὴ τοῖς στρατιώταις.
> When they arrived . . . the soldiers decided.

It is used with τις (indefinite) :

> εἰς δή τινα τόπον, to some place or other.

It is used with superlatives :

> στρατόπεδόν τε μέγιστον δὴ τοῦτο.
> This was the greatest armament.
>
> πρᾶγμα μόνον δὴ τῶν πάντων ἐλπίδος κρεῖσσον.
> The only event of all that surpassed expectation.

It is used with imperatives :

> φέρε δή, come then !

NOTE.—νῦν δή = 'just now' or 'now especially'. τότε δή = 'then especially' (*tum maxime*).

It is resumptive :

> φημὶ δὴ δεῖν εἰσφέρειν χρήματα.
> I say, then, that we must contribute money.

δή is common after γάρ preceded by an adjective or pronoun :

> πλεῖσται γὰρ δὴ αὗται ἐναυμάχησαν.
> For these ships were fighting in very large numbers.

δήπου, 'as you know' :

> οὗτοι γὰρ ἄπιστοι ἦσαν δήπου φύσει.
> For these men were naturally treacherous, as you know.

'I suppose, forsooth' (ironical) :

> σχεδὸν ἴσμεν ἅπαντες δήπου.
> Almost all of us are aware, I suppose.

οὐ γὰρ δήπου, 'for surely it cannot be' (*nisi forte*), introducing an absurd supposition. οὐ δήπου in reply to a question : 'I should think not'.

μέντοι, 'however, and yet'. οὐ μέντοι, 'certainly not' (confirmatory) :

ἀλλὰ μέντοι, ἔφη ὁ Χειρίσοφος.
'Well, for the matter of that', said Cheirisophus.

ἐν ταὐτῷ γε μέντοι ἦσθα τούτοις.
And yet surely you were present with these men.

νῦν οὖν καιρός ἐστιν ἐπιδείξασθαι τὴν παιδείαν καὶ φυλάξασθαι μέντοι.
So now is the time to display your training and to take care, withal . . .

μήν, γε μήν, καὶ μήν (καί), ἀλλὰ μήν, 'furthermore'.
οὐ μὴν ἀλλά, 'not but what', οὐ μὴν οὐδέ, 'not that' :

πάντων γε μὴν ἓν ὑπερέχει.
One thing, however, excels them all. (Strongly adversative.)

οὐ μὴν οὐδὲ βαρβάρους εἴρηκε.
He has *not* used the term Barbarians *either*.

καὶ μὴν οἱ Λακεδαιμόνιοι οὐκέτι ἔμελλον.
And in fact the Spartans did not longer delay.

καὶ μὴν εἰσὶ νόμοι.
Nay more, there are laws . . . (emphatic confirmation from a different point of view).

οὖν, 'therefore, then'; often used with μέν, δέ. δ' οὖν is resumptive ; it comes to the point, reverts from a digression, dismisses a parenthesis — 'be that as it may' :

ἐκ δ' οὖν τῆς γῆς ἀπεχώρησαν. .
At all events, they retired from the land.

τιμᾶται δ' οὖν μοι ὁ ἀνὴρ θανάτου.
Well, then, the man proposes the death penalty for me.

μὲν οὖν is transitional or resumptive :

τὸ μὲν οὖν νόσημα τοιοῦτον ἦν, such then was the plague.

ἐγὼ μὲν οὖν frequently introduces the main part of a speech or the peroration.

εἶτα, 'then, next, and consequently, and further' :

εἶτ' οὐκ αἰσχύνει; Are you not then ashamed ?
εἶτα κατηγορεῖ μὲν ἐμοῦ, and further he accuses me . . .

τοίνυν, 'well then':

> ἐπειδὴ τοίνυν ἐποιήσατο τὴν εἰρήνην ἡ πόλις.
> Since then the city made peace ...

γοῦν, 'at any rate'; explaining in what sense a preceding statement is to be taken:

(Pericles, says Thucydides, was outspoken ...)

> ὁπότε γοῦν αἴσθοιτο αὐτοὺς ὕβρει θαρσοῦντας, κατέπλησσεν.
> At any rate, when he saw the people over-elated, he used to frighten them.

> καὶ ταῖς γοῦν ναυσὶν ἐθάρσει.
> In the fleet at least he was still confident.

NOTE.—The following cannot stand first in a sentence: ἄρα, δέ, γε, γοῦν, δ' οὖν, μὲν οὖν, γάρ, μέντοι, δή, δῆτα, οὖν, τοίνυν.

ENGLISH INDEX

(*The references are to pages*)

Absolute infinitive, 67
Accompaniment, dative of, 105
Accusative absolute, 58
Accusative and infinitive, 7
Accusative and infinitive, article with, 69
Accusative and participle, 10
Accusative case, uses of, 93
Accusing, verbs of, 99
Adjectives, uses of, 71
Adverbial accusative, 95
Adverbial adjectives, 74
Adverbial participles, 60
Adverbs, uses of, 76
Agent, dative of, 106
And that, too, though, 43
Answers to questions, 5
Antecedent attraction, 54
Anticipatory accusative, 15
Aorist for perfect, 122
Aorist for pluperfect, 121
Aorist tense, uses of, 121
Apposition, 91
Article, omission of, 77
Article, uses of, 77
Article used distributively, 78
Article used pronominally, 79
Article with quotations, 78
As (comparative), 44
As (correlative), 49
As if, 48, 60
As though, 48

Brachylogy of comparison, 47

Causal clauses, 41
Cause, dative of, 104
Cause, genitive of, 96
Cognate accusative, 94
Commands, direct, 2
Commands, indirect, 13
Comparatio compendiaria, 47
Comparative clauses, 44
Complement, 88
Complexive aorist, 121
Concessive clauses, 43
Conditional participle, 60
Conditional sentences, 26
Conditions in O.O., 32
Connective relative, 55
Consecutive clauses, 23
Correlatives, 49

Dative case, uses of, 102
Dative of Reference, 63
Dative verbs, 102
Defining genitives and adverbs, 71
Definition, genitive of, 96
Deictic use of pronouns, 83
Demonstrative, attraction of, 83
Demonstrative pronouns, 82
Denying, verbs of, 17
Description, genitive of, 101
Descriptive adjectives, 75
Double comparative, 46
Doubting, verbs of, 17

Elliptic genitive, 101
Emotion, verbs of, 100

Epexegetic infinitive, 67
Epistolary aorist, 122
Epistolary perfect, 120
Ethic dative, 105
Even if, 29
Except, 28, 47
Exclamation, genitive of, 100
Exclamations, 6
Exhortations, 3

Final clauses, 21
For example, 45, 50
Forbidding, verbs of, 17
Future middles passive in meaning, 118

Genitive absolute, 61
Genitive and participle, 11
Genitive case, uses of, 96
Genitive of Comparison, 46
Genitive of Purpose, 70
Genitive with verbs, 97
Gnomic aorist, 121

Hindering, verbs of, 17
Hoping, verbs of, 9

If haply, 15, 29
Illogical comparison, 47
Imperfect tense, uses of, 120
Impersonal verbs, 57
In case, 15, 29
In the belief that, 62
Inasmuch as, 60
Indefinite pronouns, 83
Indefinite relative, 55
Infinitive, uses of, 66
Infinitive of Exclamation, 70
Infinitive of Limitation, 67
Infinitive of Purpose, 67
Infinitive with article, 68
Ingressive aorist, 121
Instrument, dative of, 105
Intensive pronoun, 80
Internal accusative, 94

Interrogative pronouns, 83
Iterative imperfect, 1, 28, 120

Know how to, 11
Knowing, verbs of, 10

Limiting apposition, 92

Manner, dative of, 104
Measure, genitive of, 96
Measure of Difference, 105
Middle voice, 116

Negative, uses of, 129
Nominative and infinitive, 7

Oaths, 95
Objective genitive, 96
On the ground that, 41, 60
One . . . another, 51
Otherwise, 28

Participle, uses of, 59
Participle of Potential, 31, 65
Participle with verbs, 61
Partitive genitive, 72, 96
Passive aorists of deponent verbs, 117
Passive voice, 116
Past tenses of indicative in O.O., 9, 14, 32
Perceiving, verbs of, 10
Perfects with present meaning, 119
Personal pronouns, 80
Possessive adjectives, 72
Possessive genitive, 96
Possessive pronouns, 81
Potential use, 1, 9, 30
Predicative adjective, 72
Predicative participle, 64
Pregnant use of prepositions, 115
Prepositions, uses of, 107
Preventing, verbs of, 17

Price, genitive of, 100
Prolative infinitive, 66
Promising, verbs of, 9
Pronouns, uses of, 80
Pronouns and Adverbs, table of, 86
Proportion, 45

Questions, deliberative, 5
Questions, direct, 3
Questions, indirect, 13

Reciprocal pronouns, 85
Reference, dative of, 104
Reflexive pronouns, 81
Relative attraction, 53
Relative clauses, 51
Relative clauses attracted in conditions, 30
Relative clauses attracted in O.O., 16
Relative for demonstrative, 55
Repeated negative, 130
Repeated relative, 52
Respect, accusative of, 95
Respect, dative of, 105
Retained accusative, 94

Space, extent of, 95
Sphere in which, genitive of, 97
Statements, direct, 1
Statements, indirect, 7
Subjective genitive, 96

Subordinate clauses in O.O., 15
Such a man as you, 49
Superlative, ways of expressing, 47
Swearing, verbs of, 9

Temporal clauses, 37
Tenses of the imperative, 122
Tenses of the indicative, 119
Tenses of the infinitive, 123
Tenses of the optative, 123
Tenses of the participle, 125
Tenses of the subjunctive, 123
Than, 45
The fact that, 69
Time, extent of, 95
Time, genitive of, 101
Time when, dative of, 106
Timeless aorist, 122
To see if, 15, 29
Too, 48, 67

Unfulfilled purpose, 21
Unfulfilled temporal clause, 38

Value, genitive of, 100
Verbal adjectives, 127
Verbs with two accusatives, 93
Virtual O.O., 15, 33

Weather, verbs of, 57, 62
Wishes, 36

GREEK INDEX

(*The references are to pages*)

ἀγγέλλω, 11
αἰσχύνομαι, 63
ἄκρος, 73
ἀλλά, 135
ἄλλο τι ἤ; 4
ἄλλος, 84
ἅμα, 59, 104
ἀμφί, 110
ἀμφότεροι, 85
ἄν, position of, 30
ἄν ἔδει, 29
ἄν iterative, 1
ἄν omitted in conditions, 29, 31
ἄν potential, 1
ἀνά, 107
ἄνευ, 109
ἀντί, 107
ἄξιος, 101
ἀπό, 108
ἄρα, 138
ἆρα; ἆρ' οὐ; ἆρα μή; 4
ἄρτι with participle, 59
ἄρχω, ἄρχομαι, 63
ἄσμενος, 74
ἅτε, 41, 60
αὐτός, 80

βούλει; 5
βουλομένῳ ἐστί, 63

γάρ, 137
γε, 138
γοῦν, 142

δ' οὖν, 141
δέ, 136

δεῖ 'there is need', 98
δεῖνα, 84
δή, 139
δῆλον ὅτι, 11
δῆλος, 58
δήπου, 140
διά, 109
δίκαιος, 58, 67
δοκεῖ μοι, 58
δοκέω, 7

ἐὰν ἄρα, εἰ ἄρα, 29
ἐὰν καί, εἰ καί, 43
ἐάν πως, εἴ πως, 15, 29
ἐάνπερ, εἴπερ, 31
εἰ δὲ μή, 28
εἰ μὴ ἄρα, 29, 138
εἰ with verbs of emotion, 11
εἴθε, εἰ γάρ, 36
εἰμι, moods of, 119, 125
εἰς, 107
εἶτα, 141
ἐκ, ἐξ, 108
ἕκαστος, 85
ἑκάτερος, 85
ἑκὼν εἶναι, 68
ἐν, 108
ἕνεκα, 115
ἔοικα, 58
ἐπεί='for', 138
ἐπί, 111
ἔστιν οἵ, 51
ἔσχατος, 73
εὐθύς with participle, 59
ἐφ' ᾧ, ἐφ' ᾧτε, 23
ἔχω with adverb, 76

GREEK PROSE USAGE

ἔχω with infinitive, 67
ἕως, 38

ἤ comparative, 45
ἤ in double questions, 4
ἦ μήν, 10
ἤ omitted in comparison, 46
ἡγέομαι, 98
ἥμισυς, 74, 96

θαυμάζω, 12, 120
θαυμαστὸς ὅσος, 52

ἵνα ἄν, 21
ἵνα final, 21
ἵνα τί; 4
ἵνα with past indicative, 30
ἴσος, 45, 104

καθάπερ, 44, 91
καί, 132
καὶ ἐάν, 43
καὶ πῶς; 5
καίπερ, 43
κἂν εἰ, 43
κατά, 109
κινδυνεύω, 19, 66
κωλύω, 17

λαθών, 62
λανθάνω, 61, 62, 64, 122, 125
λοιπός, 96

μά, 95
μέλλω, 66, 119
μέν, 136
μὲν οὖν, 141
μέντοι, 141
μέσος, 73
μετά, 110
μεταξύ with participle, 59
μέχρι, 114
μή in cautious assertions, 2
μή in direct commands, 2
μή in indirect statements, 129

μὴ ὅτι, 135
μὴ οὔ, 17, 18, 19
μὴ πολλάκις, 20
μή with infinitive, 9, 129
μή with participle, 59, 60, 130
μή with verbs of fearing, 19
μή with verbs of hindering, 17
μή with verbs of precaution, 18
μήν, 141
μῶν; 4

νή, 95

ὁ αὐτός, 45
οἷα δή, 60
οἶδ' ὅτι, 11
οἷον, 45, 50, 60
οἱόνπερ, 48
οἷος, 24, 49
ὅλος, 73
ὅμοιος, 45, 104
ὅπως comparative, 44
ὅπως final, 21
ὅπως in commands, 3, 18
ὅπως in precautions, 18
ὅς γε, 41, 55, 139
ὅσα μή, 65, 131
ὅσον ' about ', 50
ὅσον consecutive, 25
ὅσον οὔ, 131
ὅστις consecutive, 54, 55
ὅστις ' in that he ', 41, 55
ὁστισοῦν, 84
ὅτε, 39
ὅτι, 8, 9, 10, 41
ὅτι μή, 131
ὅτι with superlatives, 75
οὐ μή, 3
οὐδέ, μηδέ, 134
οὐδεὶς ὅστις οὔ, 51
οὐδὲν ἄλλο ἤ, 84
οὐκ ἄν μοι δοκῶ, 33
οὐκ ἂν οἶδα εἰ, 30
οὐκ ἂν φθάνοις, 63

GREEK PROSE USAGE

οὐκ ἀξιόω, 13
οὐκ ἐάω, 13
οὐκ ἔσθ' ὅπως, 51
οὐκοῦν, 5
οὔκουν, 5
οὖν, 141
οὔτε, μήτε, 134
οὑτοσί, 83
οὐχ ὅπως, 135
οὐχ ὅσπερ, 45
οὐχ ὅτι, 135

πάλαι and imperfect, 120
πάλαι with present, 119
παρά, 112
πᾶς, 73
περί, 112
περιοράω, 65
ποιοῦμαι in periphrases, 117
πολλοῦ δεῖν, 67
πότερον; 4
ποῦ τῆς γῆς; 96
πρίν, 39
πρό, 108
πρός, 113
πρῶτος, 74
πῶς καί; 5
πῶς οὐ; 4

σκοταῖος, 74
σύν, 108
συνελών, 68
σφέτερος, 82

τε inferential, 133
τε . . . καί, 133

τε . . . τε, 134
τὸ μή with verbs of preventing, 17
τοίνυν, 142
τοῦ μή final, 70
τοῦ μή with verbs of preventing, 17
τυγχάνω, 61, 62, 64, 122, 125

ὑπέρ, 110
ὑπό, 114
ὕστερος ' too late ', 46

φαίνομαι, 63
φανερός, 58
φθάνω, 61, 122, 125
φθάσας, 62

χωρίς, 109

ὡς comparative, 44
ὡς consecutive, 25
ὡς ἔπος εἰπεῖν, 68
ὡς final, 21
ὡς in exclamations, 6
ὡς temporal, 39
ὡς with participle, 41, 60
ὡς with positive adverbs, 52, 76
ὡς with superlatives, 75
ὥσπερ ἂν εἰ, 48
ὥσπερ comparative, 44
ὥσπερ εἰ, 30, 48
ὥσπερ with participle, 60
ὥστε, 23
ὤφελον, 36

THE END